FIRST 50
EARLY ROCK SONGS
YOU SHOULD PLAY ON THE PIANO

ISBN 978-1-4950-6495-1

HAL•LEONARD®
CORPORATION
7777 W. BLUEMOUND RD. P.O. BOX 13819 MILWAUKEE, WI 53213

Visit Hal Leonard Online at
www.halleonard.com

CONTENTS

AIN'T THAT A SHAME

Words and Music by ANTOINE DOMINO
and DAVE BARTHOLOMEW

Moderate Swing

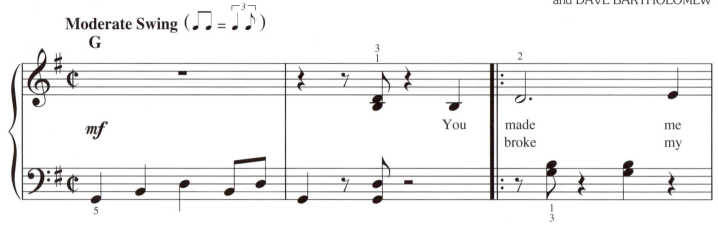

blame. _____ You / Oh well, good - bye, al -

though I'll cry. Ain't that a shame! _____

My tears fell like rain. _____ Ain't that a shame! _____

You're the one to blame. _____

ARE YOU SINCERE

Words and Music by WAYNE WALKER
and LUCKY MOELLER

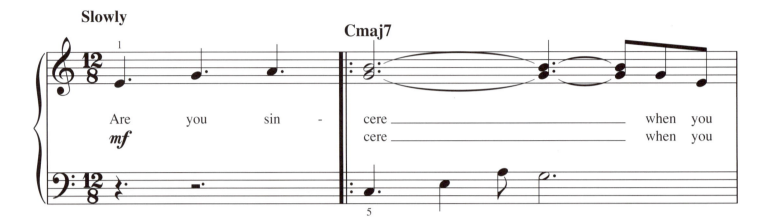

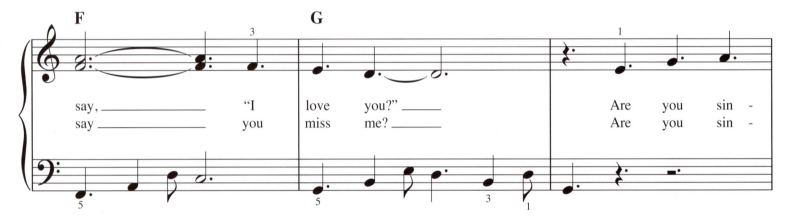

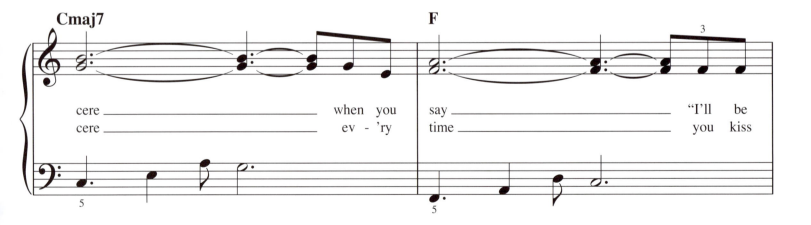

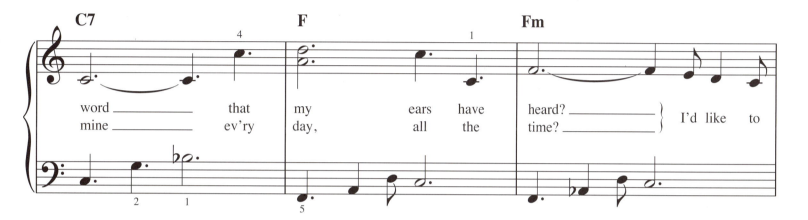

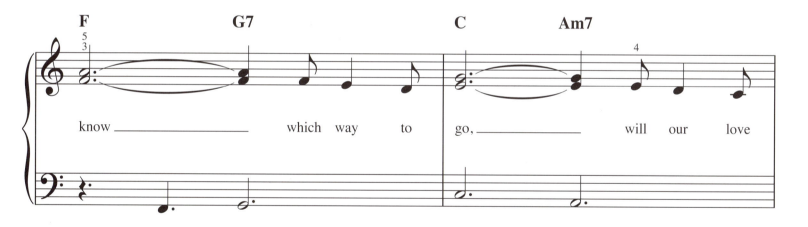

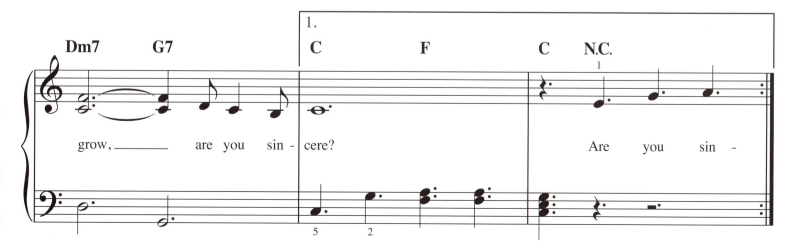

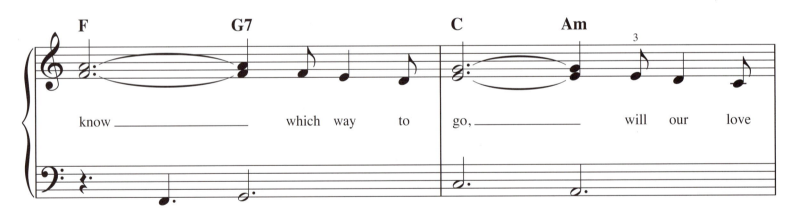

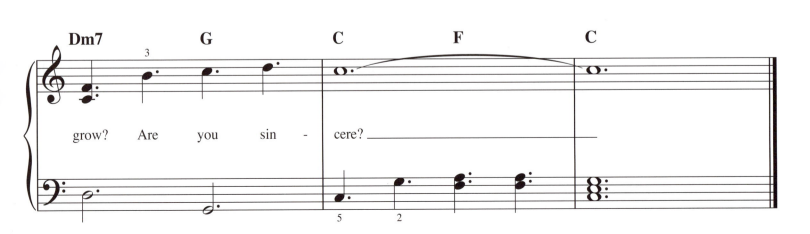

AT THE HOP

Words and Music by ARTHUR SINGER,
JOHN MADARA and DAVID WHITE

With a Rock 'n' Roll beat

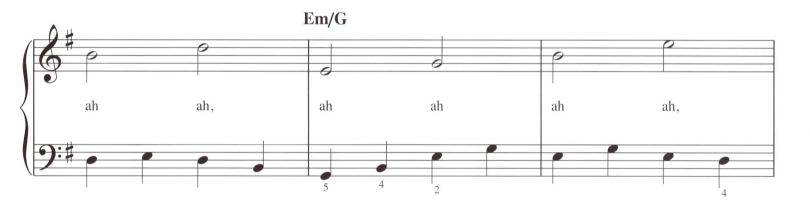

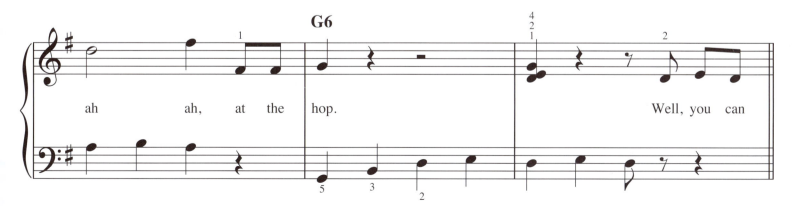

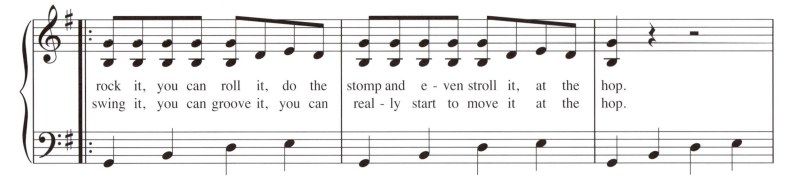

rock it, you can roll it, do the stomp and e - ven stroll it, at the hop.
swing it, you can groove it, you can real - ly start to move it at the hop.

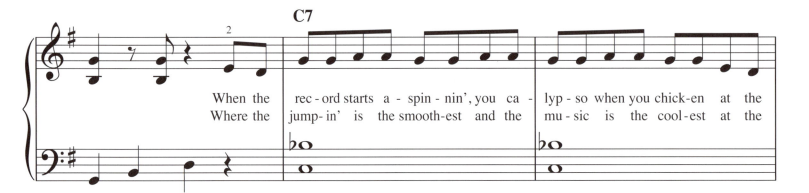

When the rec - ord starts a - spin - nin', you ca - lyp - so when you chick-en at the
Where the jump-in' is the smooth-est and the mu - sic is the cool-est at the

hop.
hop.

Do the dance sen - sa - tion that is
All the cats and chicks _____ can _____

sweep-ing the na - tion at the hop.)
get _____ their kicks, _____ at the hop.)

(Spoken:)
Let's go!

Let's go to the hop! (Oh, ba - by.) Let's go to the hop!

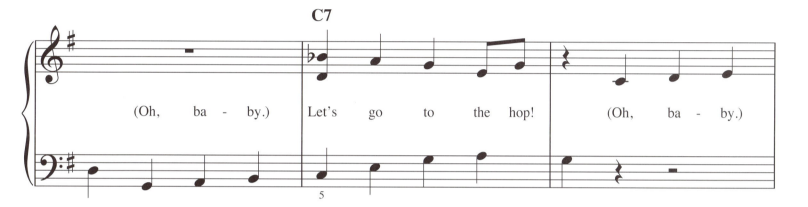

C7

(Oh, ba - by.) Let's go to the hop! (Oh, ba - by.)

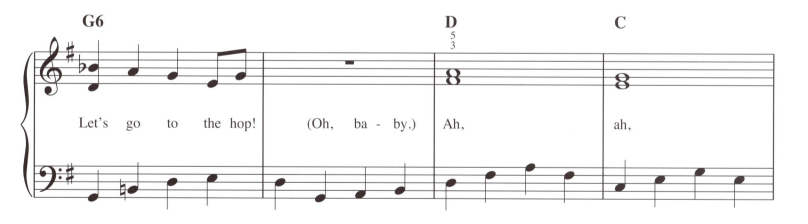

G6   **D**   **C**

Let's go to the hop! (Oh, ba - by.) Ah,   ah,

1. **G6**

let's go to the hop!   Well, you can

2. **G6**

let's go to the hop!

BIRD DOG

Words and Music by
BOUDLEAUX BRYANT

Moderately

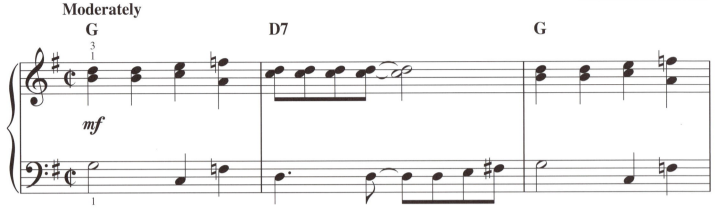

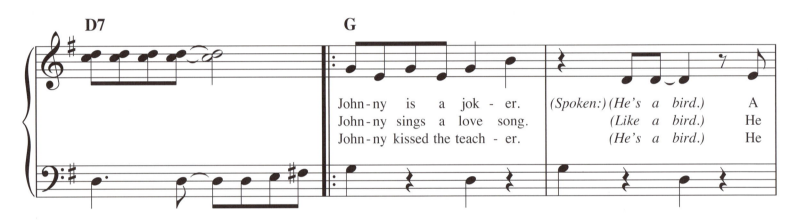

Johnny is a jok - er.
John - ny sings a love song.
John - ny kissed the teach - er.

(Spoken:)(He's a bird.) A
(Like a bird.) He
(He's a bird.) He

ver - y fun - ny jok - er.
sings the sweet - est love song.
tip - toed up to reach her.

(He's a bird.) But
(You ever heard.) But
(He's a bird.) Well,

when he jokes my hon - ey
when he sings to my gal
he's the teach-er's pet now.

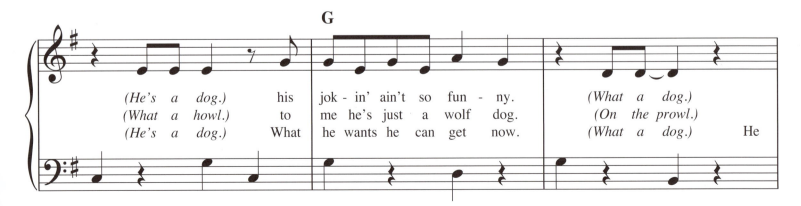

(He's a dog.) his
(What a howl.) to
(He's a dog.) What

jok - in' ain't so fun - ny.
me he's just a wolf dog.
he wants he can get now.

(What a dog.)
(On the prowl.)
(What a dog.) He

John - ny is the jok - er that's a - try - in' to steal my ba - by. *(He's a   bird   dog.)*
John - ny wants to fly a - way and pup - py love my ba - by. *(He's a   bird   dog.)*
e - ven made the teach - er let him sit next to my ba - by. *(He's a   bird   dog.)*

Hey, bird dog, get a - way from my quail.

Hey, bird dog, you're on the wrong trail.   Bird dog, you'd bet - ter leave my

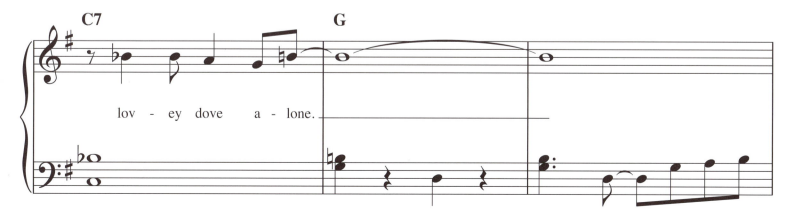

lov - ey dove a - lone.

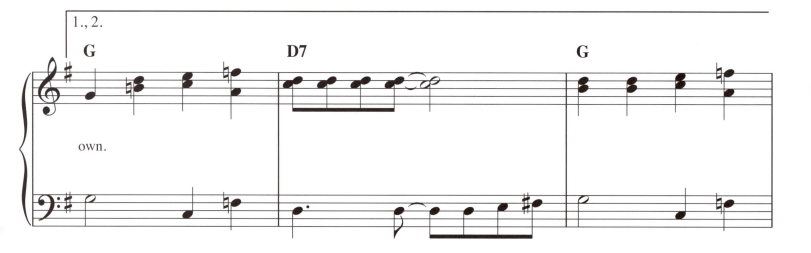

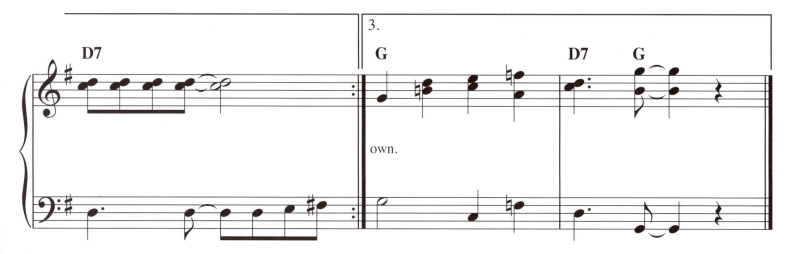

BE-BOP-A-LULA

Words and Music by TEX DAVIS
and GENE VINCENT

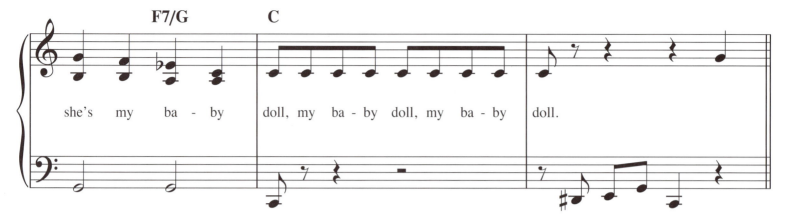

she's my ba - by doll, my ba - by doll, my ba - by doll.

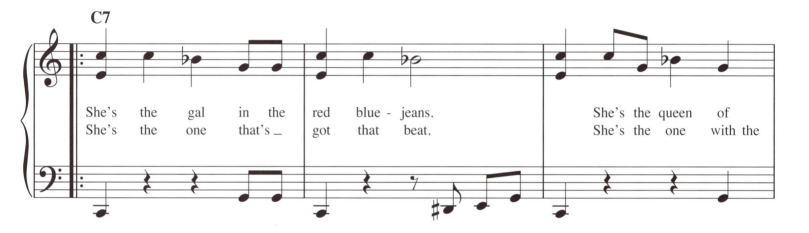

She's the gal in the red blue - jeans.
She's the one that's __ got that beat.
She's the queen of
She's the one with the

all the teens.
fly - in' feet.
She's the one _____ that I know.
She's the one that walks a - round the store.

She's the one that loves me so.
She's the one that gets more and more.
Be - bop - a - lu - la,

she's my ba - by. Be - bop - a - lu - la, I don't mean may - be.

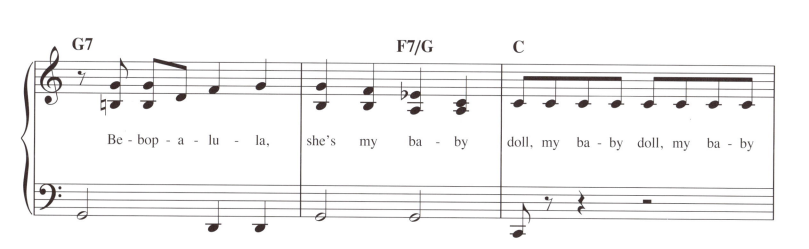

Be - bop - a - lu - la, she's my ba - by doll, my ba - by doll, my ba - by

1. doll. 2. doll. Be - bop - a - lu - la,

she's my ba - by doll, my ba - by doll, my ba - by doll.

BLUE MONDAY

Words and Music by ANTOINE "FATS" DOMINO
and DAVE BARTHOLOMEW

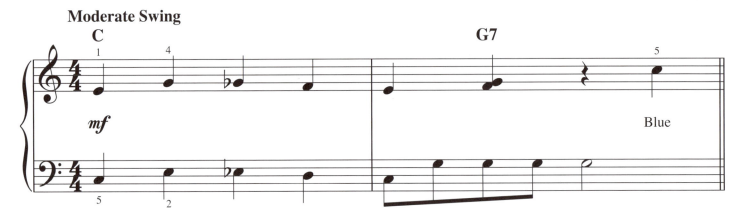

Blue

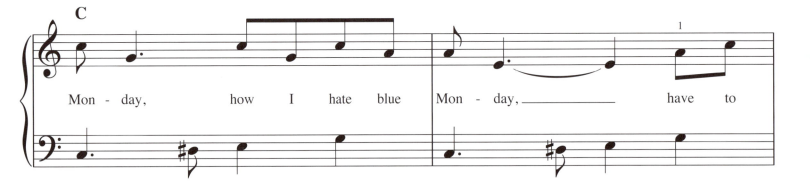

Mon - day, how I hate blue Mon - day, _____ have to

work like a slave all day. Here comes Tues - day, _____ oh hard

Tues - day, _____ I'm so tired, I've got no time to play. _____ Here comes

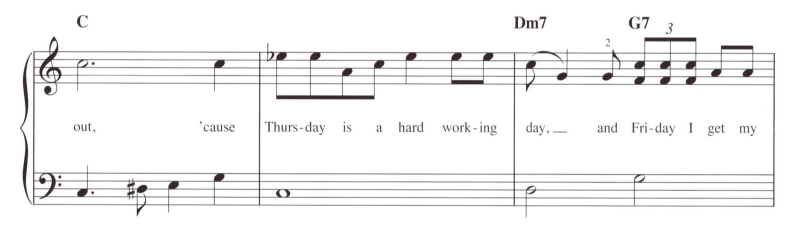

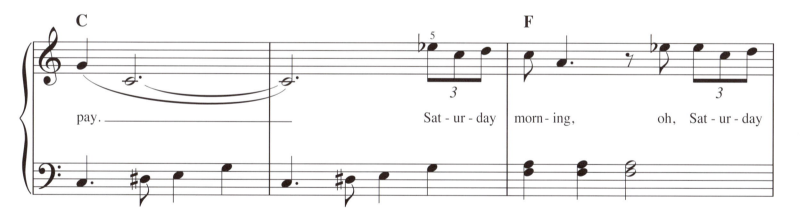

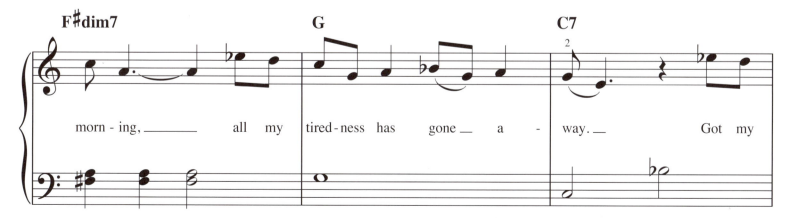

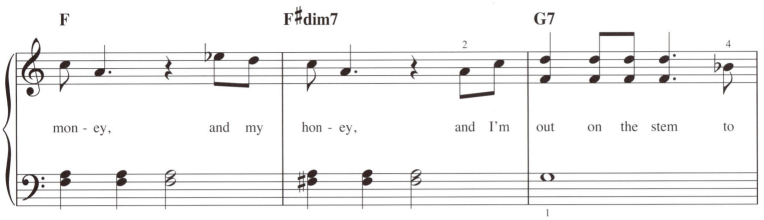

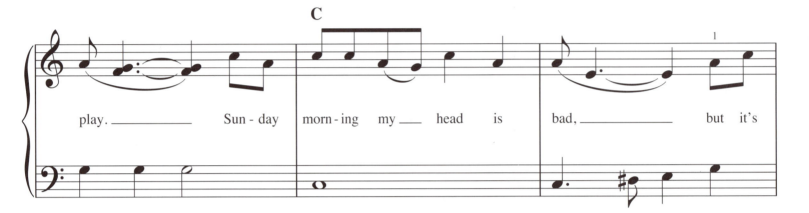

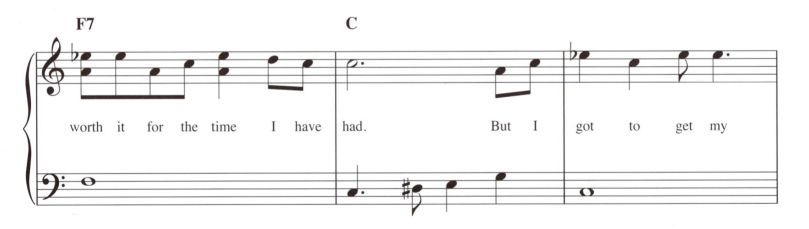

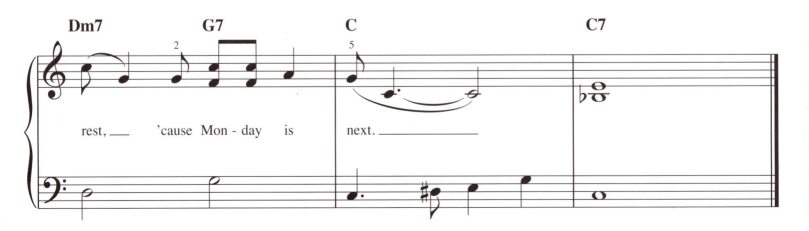

BLUE SUEDE SHOES

Words and Music by
CARL LEE PERKINS

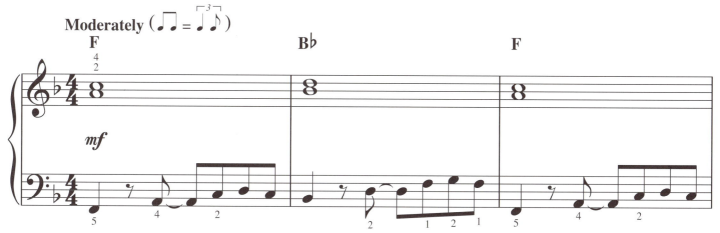

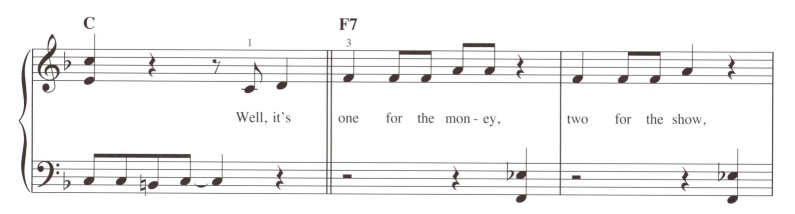

Well, it's one for the mon-ey, two for the show,

three to get read-y, now go, cat, go. But don't you

step on my blue suede shoes. You can

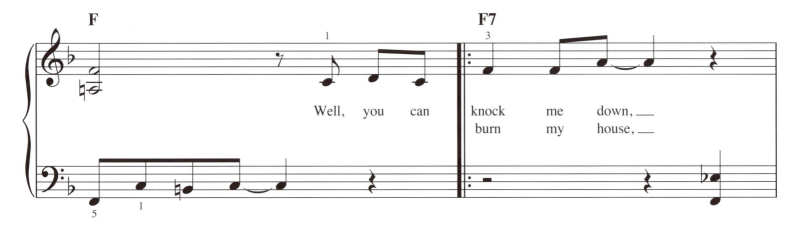

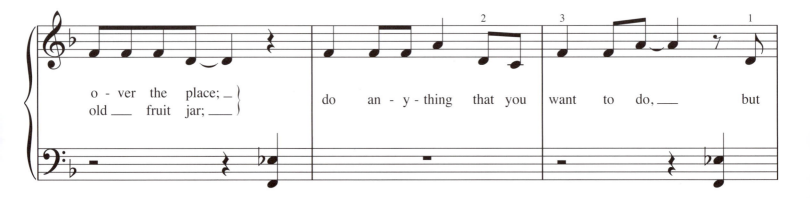

uh   uh,   hon - ey,   lay   off   of   my   shoes. _   Don't   you

step   on   my   blue   suede   shoes.   You   can

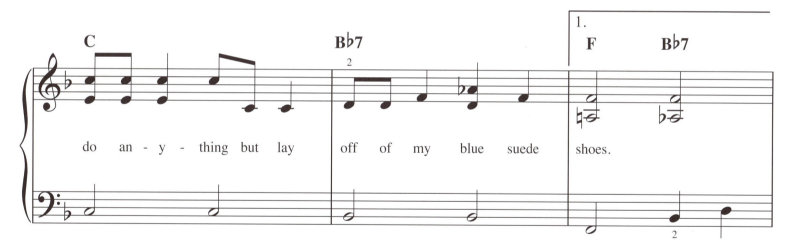

do   an - y - thing   but   lay   off   of   my   blue   suede   shoes.

Well,   you   can   shoes.

DON'T

Words and Music by JERRY LEIBER
and MIKE STOLLER

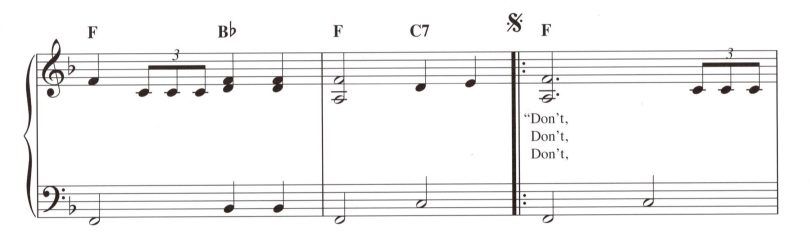

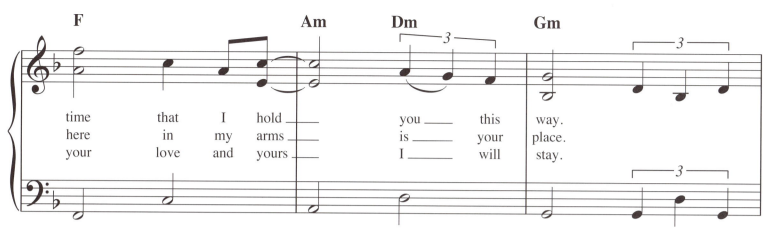

time that I hold you ___ this way.
here in my arms ___ is ___ your place.
your love and yours ___ I ___ will stay.

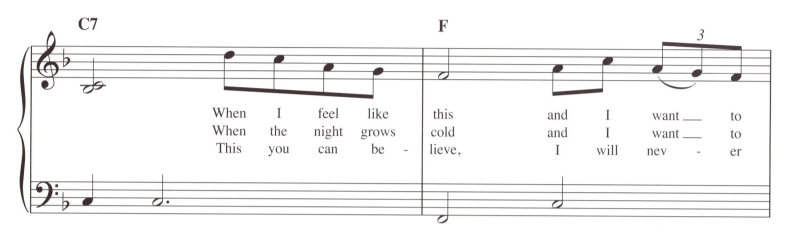

When I feel like this and I want ___ to
When the night grows cold and I want ___ to
This you can be - lieve, I will nev - er

To Coda

1.

kiss you, ba - by don't say "don't."
hold you, ba - by don't say
leave you. Heav - en knows I

2.

"don't."

If you think that

this is just a game   I'm play - ing, _____

if you think that   I don't mean ___   ev - 'ry word I'm

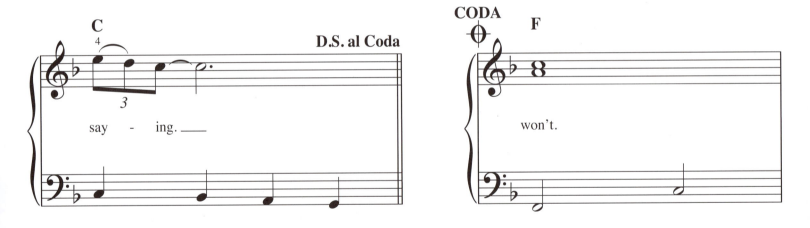

say - ing. ___   **D.S. al Coda**   **CODA**   won't.

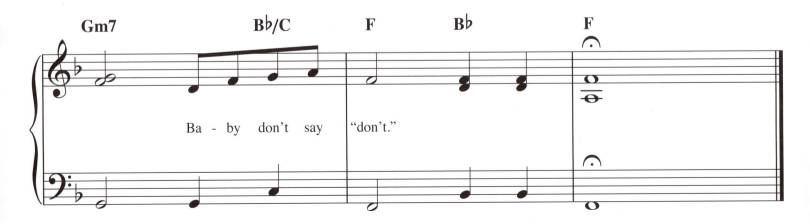

Ba - by don't say "don't."

BOOK OF LOVE

Words and Music by WARREN DAVIS,
GEORGE MALONE and CHARLES PATRICK

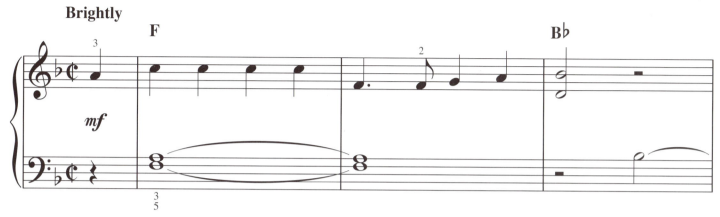

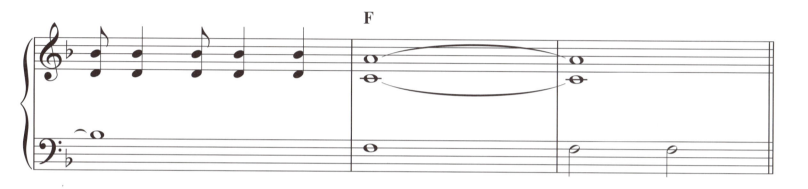

Tell me, tell me, tell me, oh, who wrote the book of

love? I've got to know the an - swer. Was it

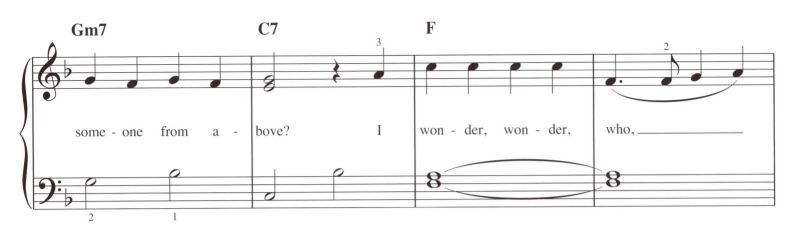

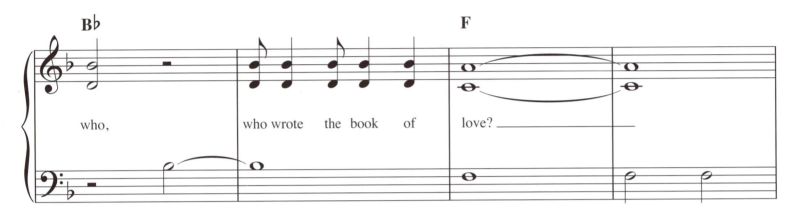

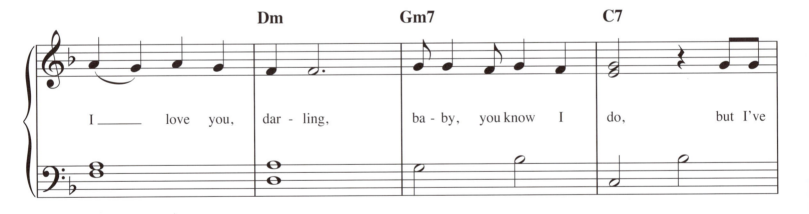

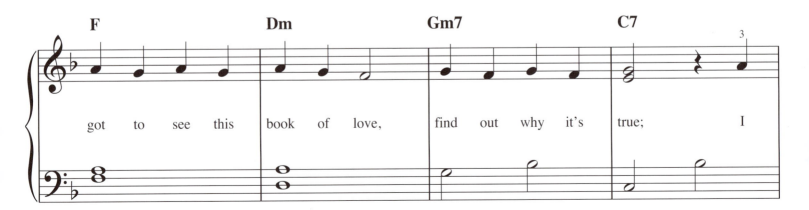

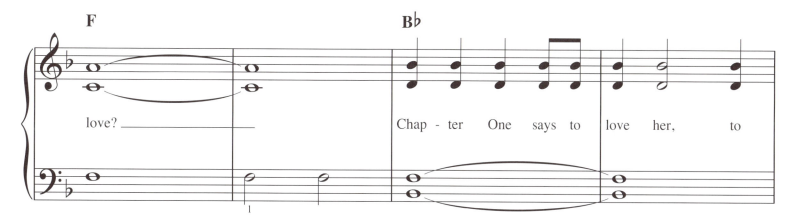

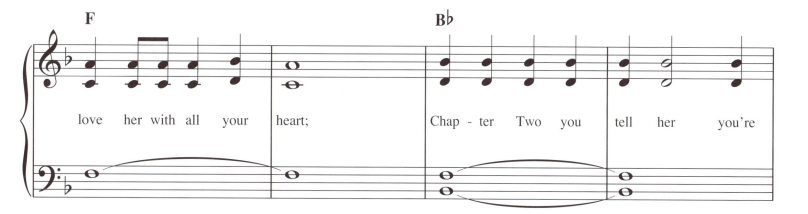

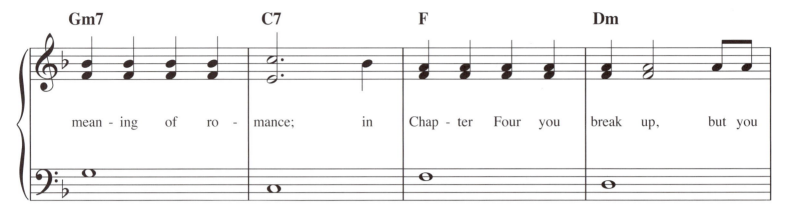

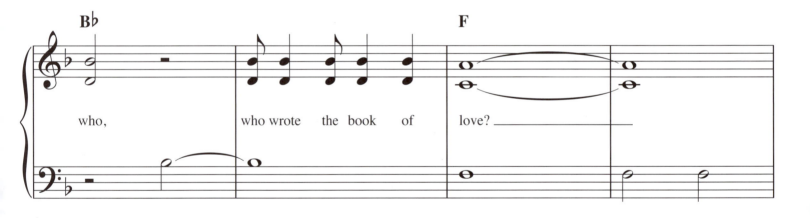

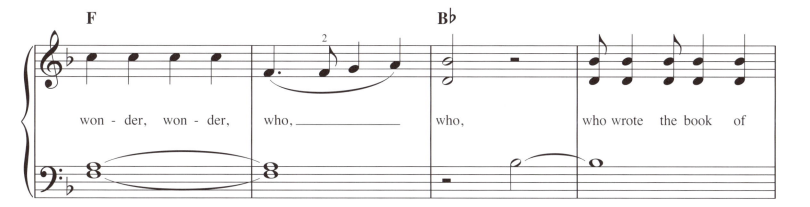

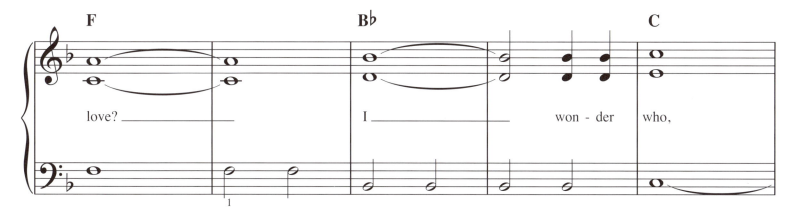

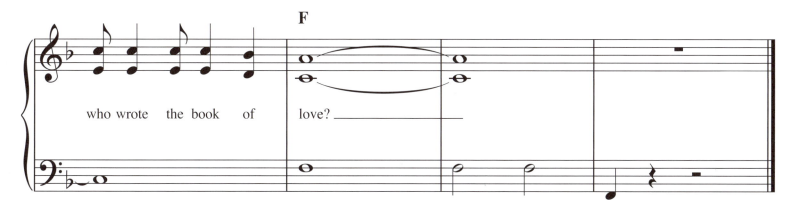

DO WAH DIDDY DIDDY

Words and Music by JEFF BARRY
and ELLIE GREENWICH

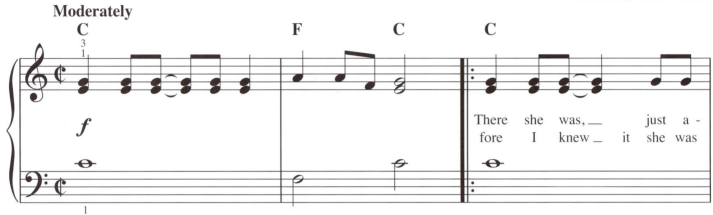

There she was, __ just a-
fore I knew __ it she was

walk - in' down the street, sing - in' do wah did - dy did - dy
walk - in' next to me, sing - in' do wah did - dy did - dy

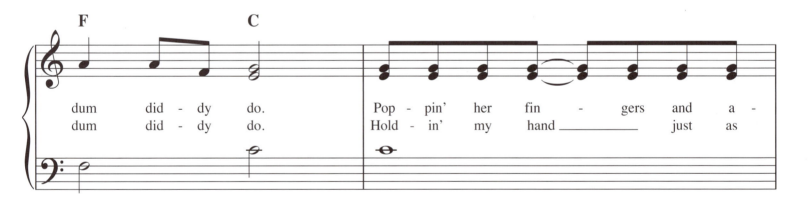

dum did - dy do. Pop - pin' her fin - gers and a-
dum did - dy do. Hold - in' my hand _____ just as

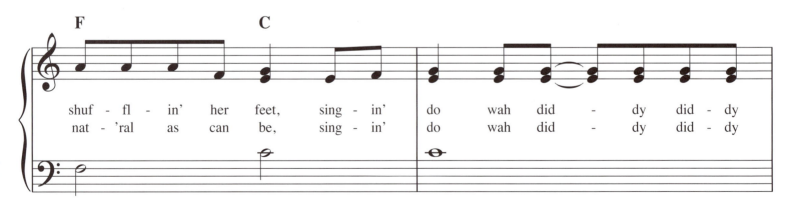

shuf - fl - in' her feet, sing - in' do wah did - dy did - dy
nat - 'ral as can be, sing - in' do wah did - dy did - dy

dum did - dy do. She looked
dum did - dy do. We walked
good, (looked good) she looked
on, (walked on) to my

fine. (Looked fine.) She looked
door. (My door.) We walked
good, she looked fine, and I
on to my door, and she

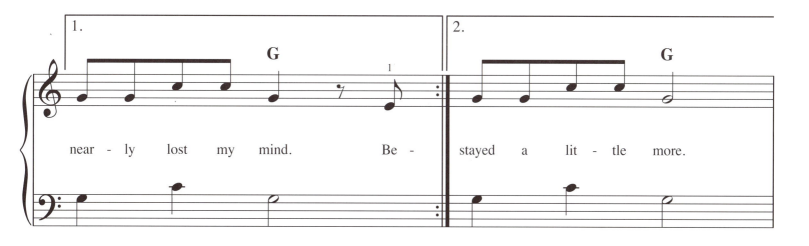

1.
near - ly lost my mind. Be -

2.
stayed a lit - tle more.

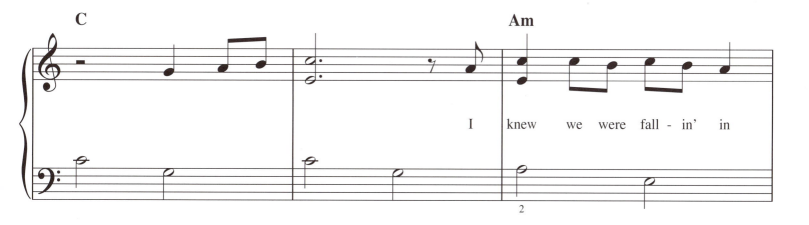

I knew we were fall - in' in

love.
I

told her all the things I was dream - in' of. ___ Now we're to - geth - er near - ly

ev - 'ry sin - gle day, sing - in' do wah did - dy did - dy dum did - dy do.

We're so hap - py and that's how we're gon - na stay, sing - in' do wah did - dy did - dy

dum did - dy do. 'Cause I'm | hers, (I'm hers) and she's | mine. (She's mine.) Well, I'm

hers and she's mine. Wed-ding | bells are gon - na chime. | Oo. _____

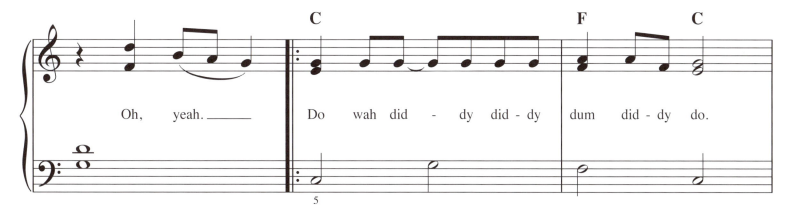

Oh, yeah. _____ | Do wah did - dy did-dy | dum did-dy do.

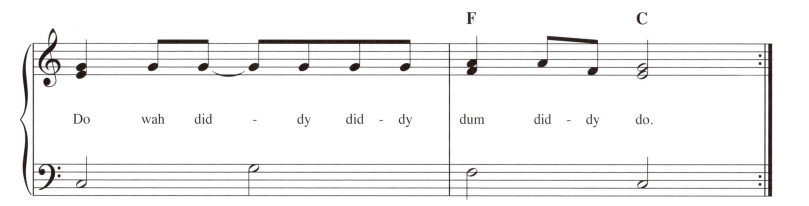

Do wah did - dy did-dy | dum did-dy do.

EVERYDAY

Words and Music by NORMAN PETTY
and CHARLES HARDIN

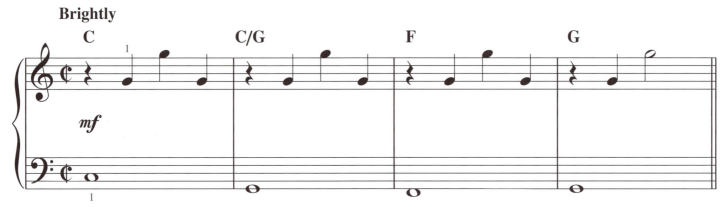

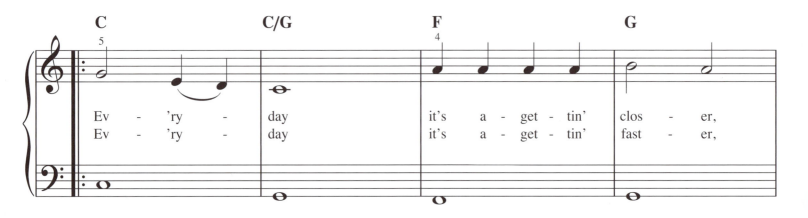

Ev - 'ry - day it's a - get - tin' clos - er,
Ev - 'ry - day it's a - get - tin' fast - er,

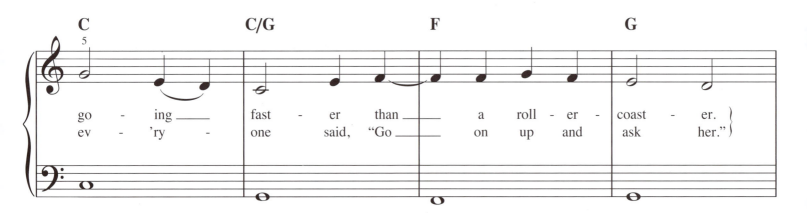

go - ing ___ fast - er than ___ a roll - er - coast - er.
ev - 'ry - one said, "Go ___ on up and ask her."

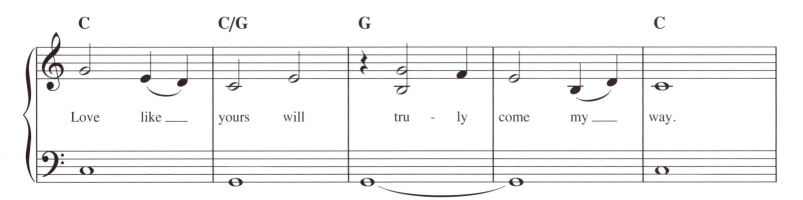

Love like ___ yours will tru - ly come my ___ way.

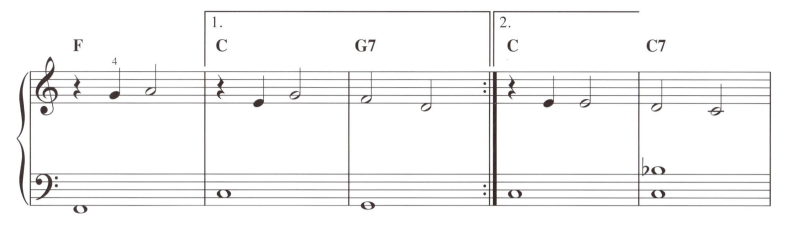

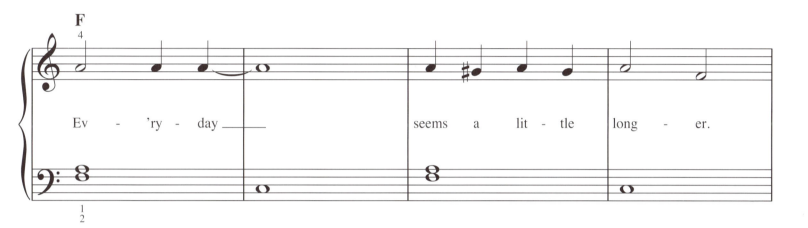

Ev - 'ry - day ____ seems a lit - tle long - er.

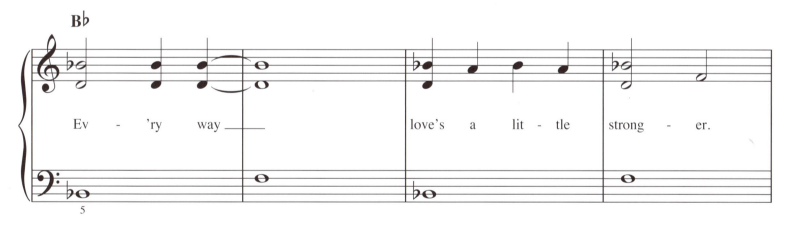

Ev - 'ry way ____ love's a lit - tle strong - er.

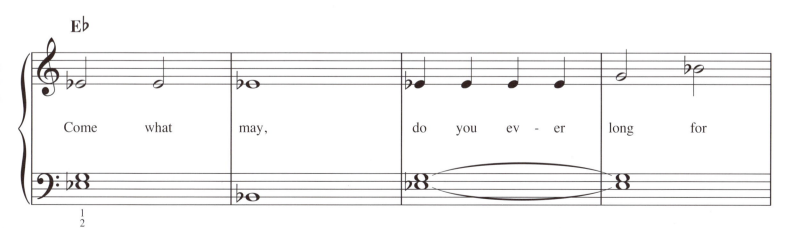

Come what may, do you ev - er long for

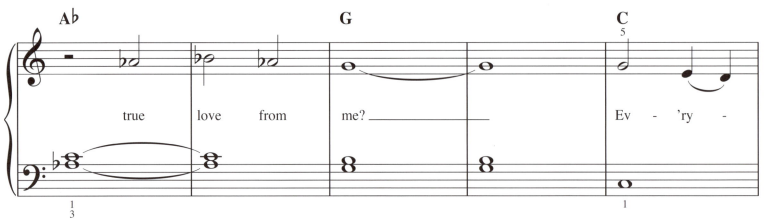

true love from me? Ev - 'ry -

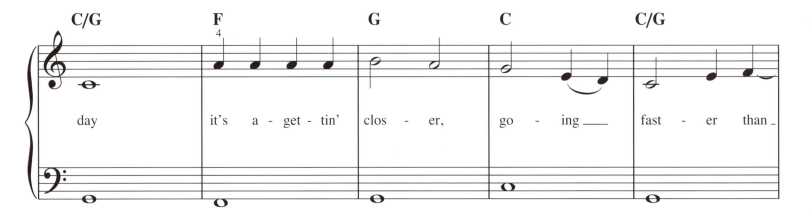

day it's a - get - tin' clos - er, go - ing ___ fast - er than ___

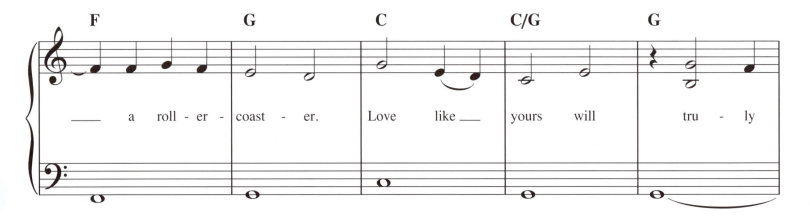

___ a roll - er - coast - er. Love like ___ yours will tru - ly

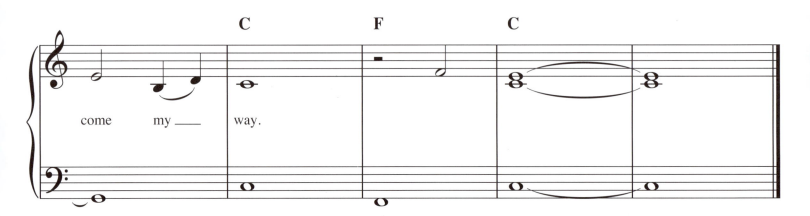

come my ___ way.

EARTH ANGEL

Words and Music by
JESSE BELVIN

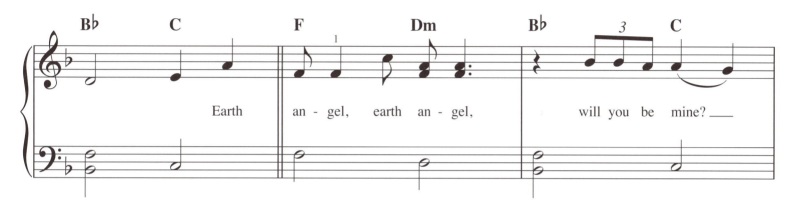

Earth an - gel, earth an - gel, will you be mine? ___

My darl-ing, dear, ___ love you ___ all the time. ___ I'm just a fool, ___

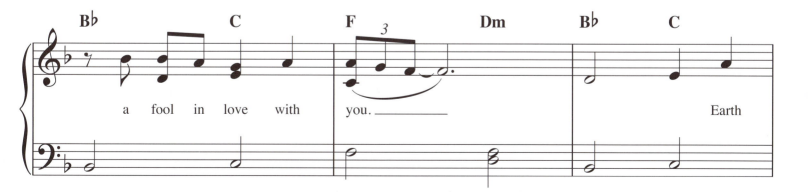

a fool in love with you. ___ Earth

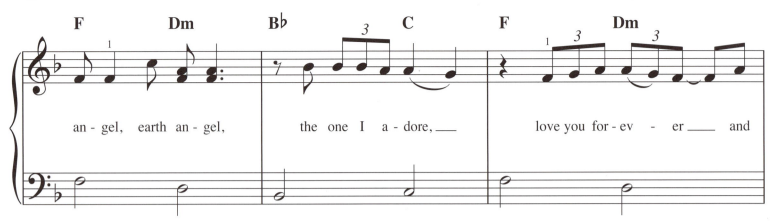

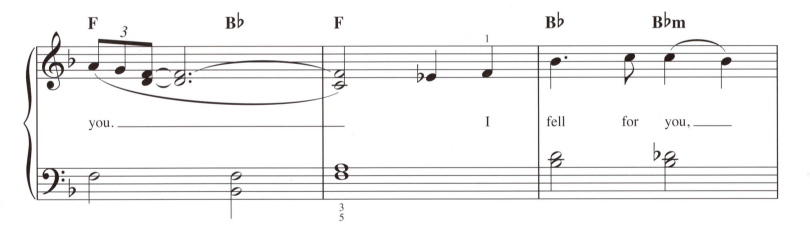

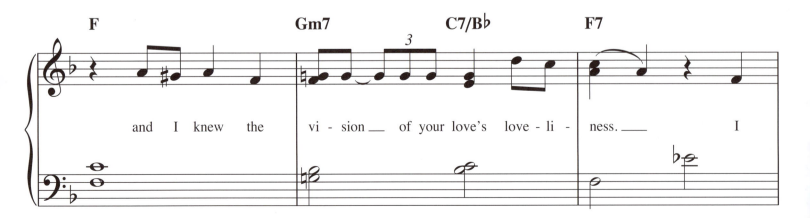

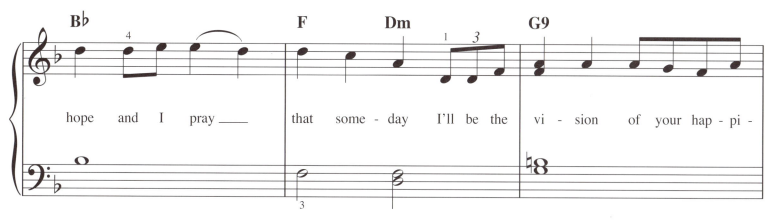

hope and I pray ____ that some-day I'll be the vi - sion of your hap-pi -

ness. Earth an - gel, earth an - gel, please be mine? ____

My darl-ing, dear, ____ love you ____ all the time. ____ I'm just a fool, ____

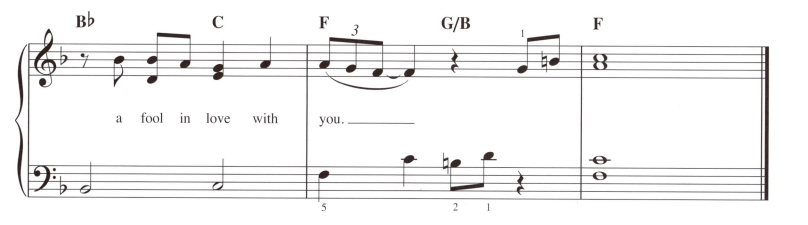

a fool in love with you. ____

THE GREAT PRETENDER

Words and Music by
BUCK RAM

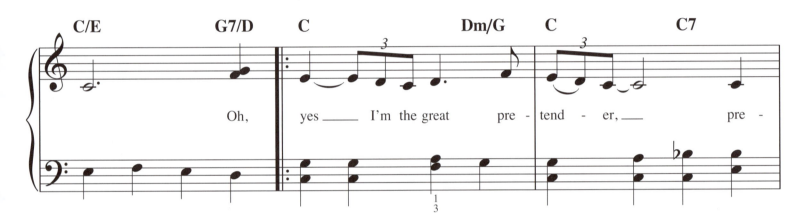

Oh, yes ___ I'm the great pre - tend - er, ___ pre -

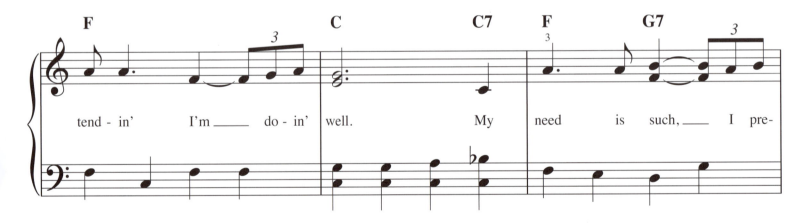

tend - in' I'm ___ do - in' well. My need is such, ___ I pre-

tend too much, I'm lone - ly but no ___ one can tell. Oh,

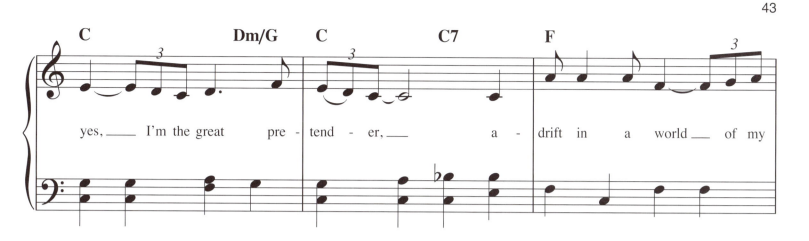

yes, ___ I'm the great pre - tend - er, ___ a - drift in a world ___ of my

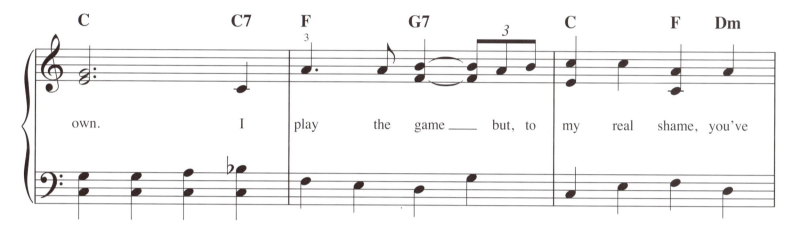

own. I play the game ___ but, to my real shame, you've

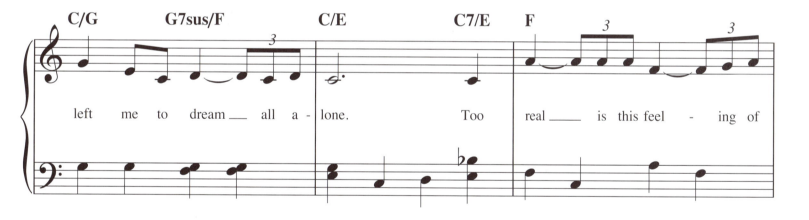

left me to dream ___ all a - lone. Too real ___ is this feel - ing of

make - be - lieve, too real ___ when I feel ___ what my

heart ___ can't con-ceal. Oh, ___ yes, ___ I'm the great pre - tend - er, ___ just

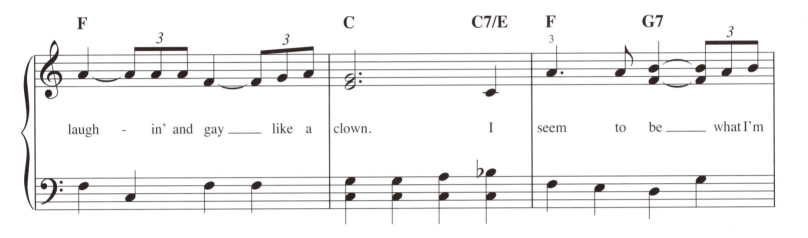

laugh - in' and gay ___ like a clown. I seem to be ___ what I'm

not, you see, I'm wear-in' my heart ___ like a crown; pre -

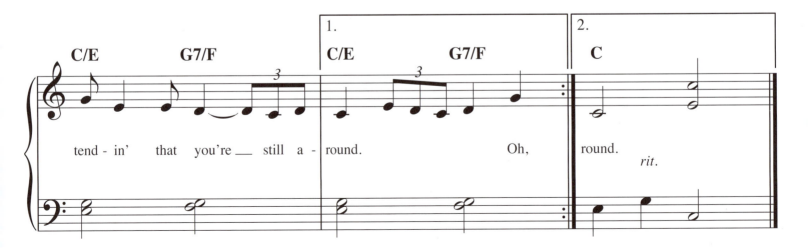

tend - in' that you're ___ still a - round. Oh, round.

rit.

HEARTBREAK HOTEL

Words and Music by MAE BOREN AXTON,
TOMMY DURDEN and ELVIS PRESLEY

Since my ba-by left me, I found a new place to dwell. Well, it's
if your ba-by leaves ya, and you've got a tale to tell, well, just

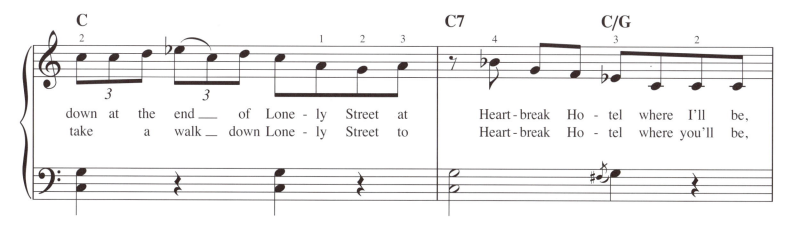

down at the end of Lone-ly Street at Heart-break Ho-tel where I'll be,
take a walk down Lone-ly Street to Heart-break Ho-tel where you'll be,

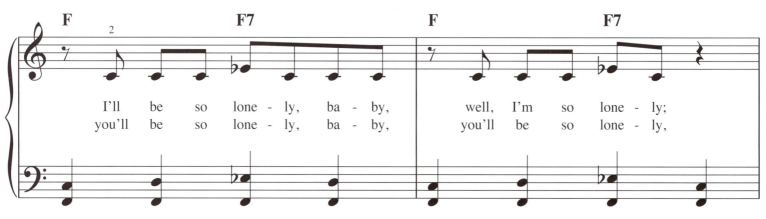

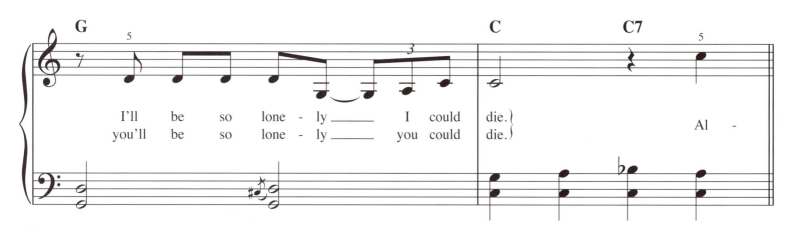

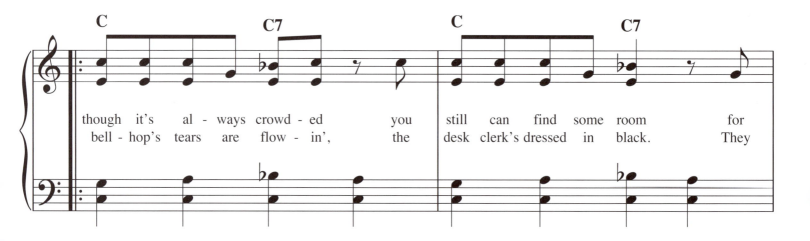

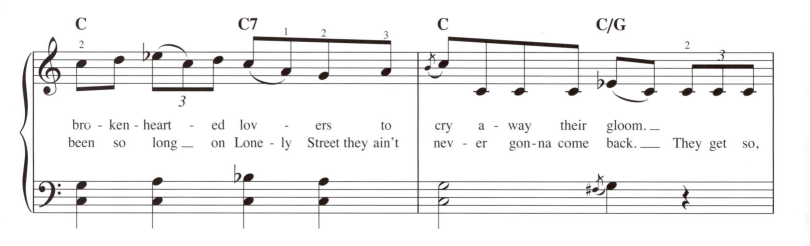

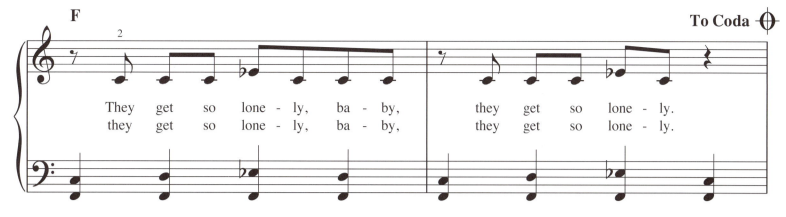

To Coda ⊕

F

They get so lone - ly, ba - by,   they get so lone - ly.
they get so lone - ly, ba - by,   they get so lone - ly.

G   **1.** **C**   **C/G**

They're so lone - ly they could   die.   Well, the
They're so lone - ly they could

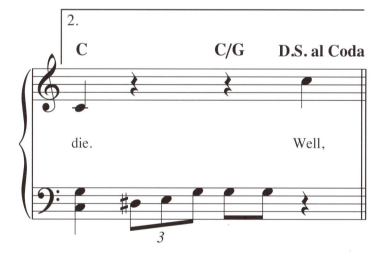

2. **C**   **C/G**   **D.S. al Coda**

die.   Well,

CODA ⊕   **G**

They're so lone - ly they could

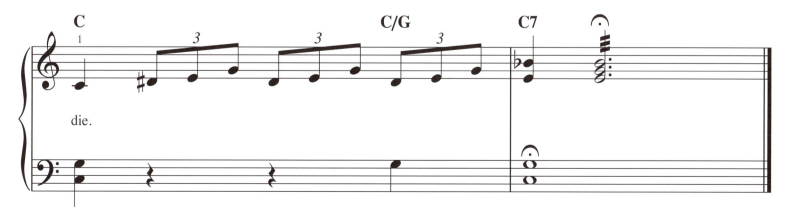

C   **C/G**   **C7**

die.

HELLO MARY LOU

Words and Music by GENE PITNEY
and C. MANGIARACINA

With a steady beat

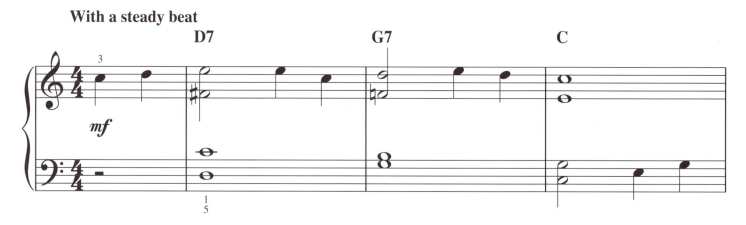

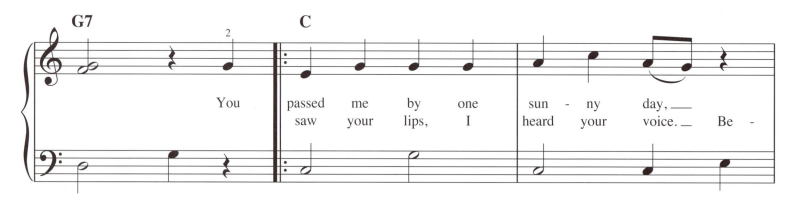

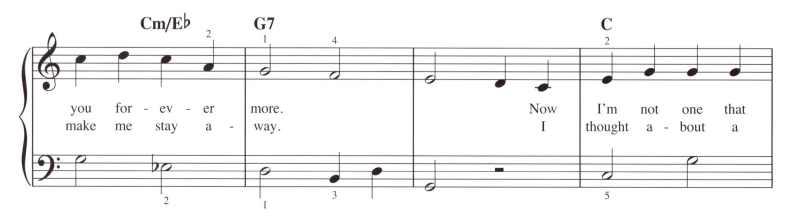

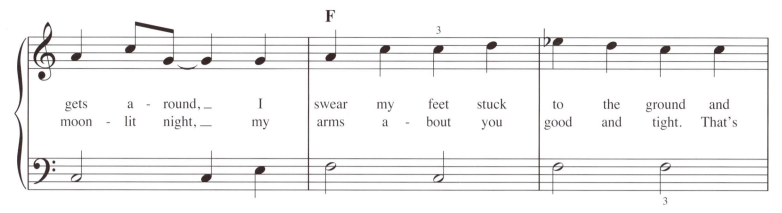

gets a - round, _ I
moon - lit night, _ my

swear my feet stuck
arms a - bout you

to the ground and
good and tight. That's

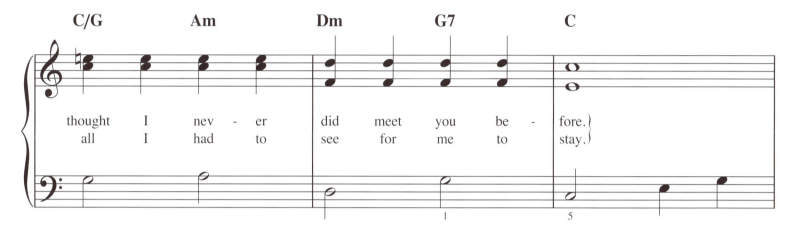

C/G   **Am**   **Dm**   **G7**   **C**

thought I nev - er
all I had to

did meet you be -
see for me to

fore.}
stay.}

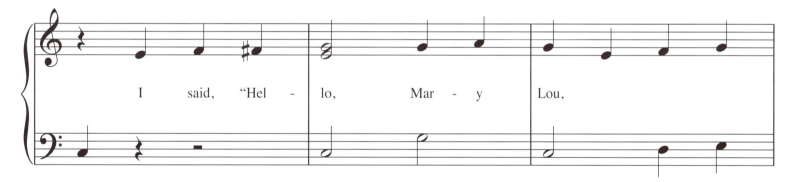

I said, "Hel - lo,   Mar - y   Lou,

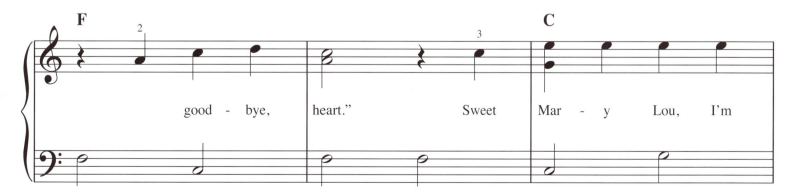

F   **C**

good - bye,   heart."   Sweet   Mar - y   Lou, I'm

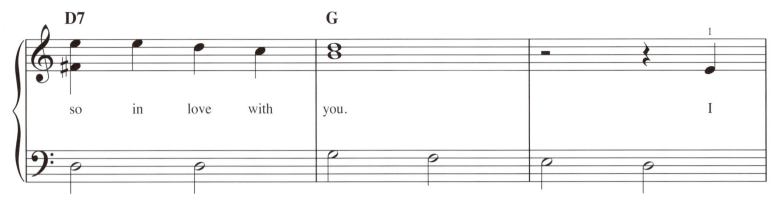

so   in   love   with   you.   I

knew,   Mar - y   Lou,   we'd   nev - er

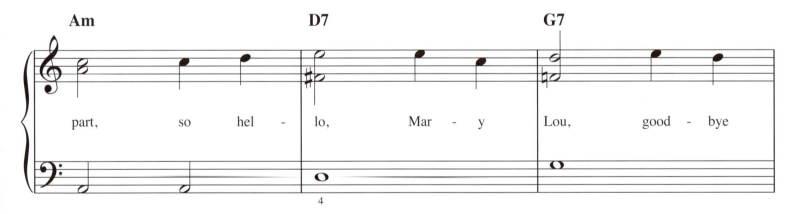

part,   so   hel - lo,   Mar - y   Lou,   good - bye

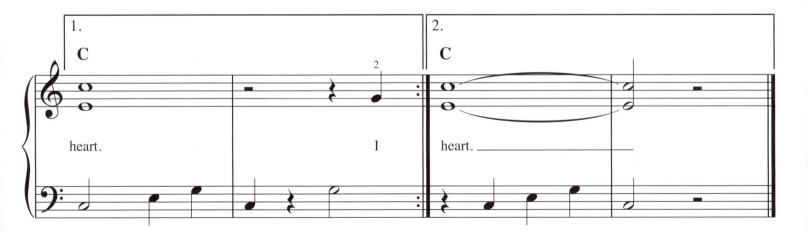

heart.   I   heart. _____

LA BAMBA

By RITCHIE VALENS

Moderate Latin rhythm

Pa - ra bai - lar la bam - ba.

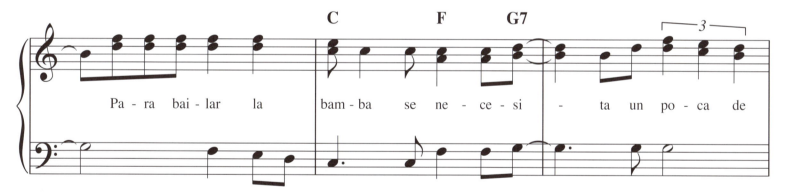

Pa - ra bai - lar la bam - ba se ne - ce - si - ta un po - ca de

gra - cia. Un - a po - ca de gra - cia para mi para ti

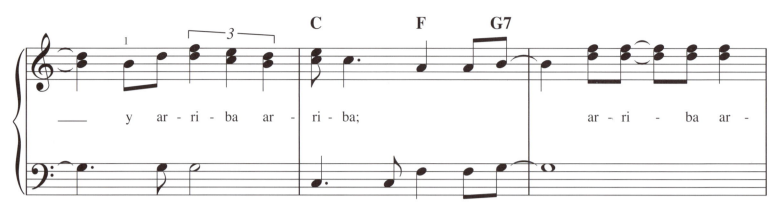

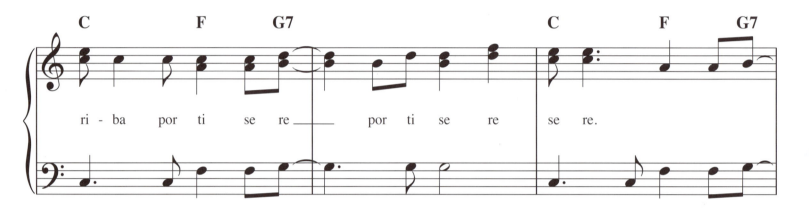

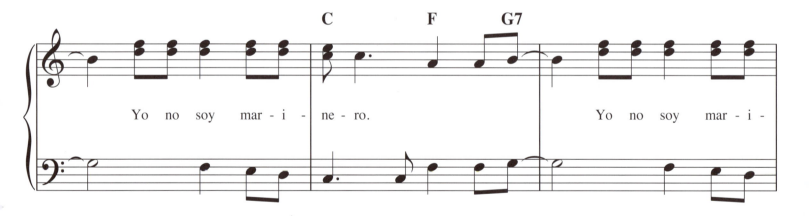

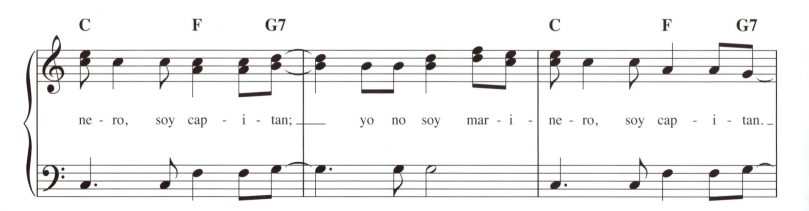

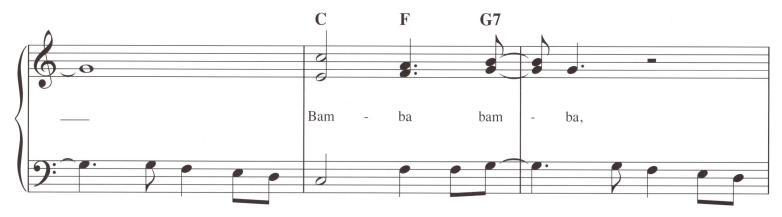

Bam - ba bam - ba,

bam - ba bam - ba, | bam - ba bam -

1.

- ba, | bam - ba bam... Pa - ra bai - lar la

2.

bam - ba bam - ba...

HUSH-A-BYE

Words by MORT SHUMAN
Music by DOC POMUS

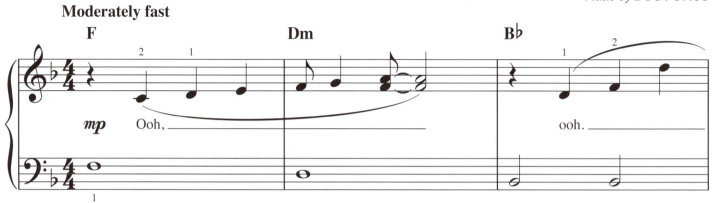

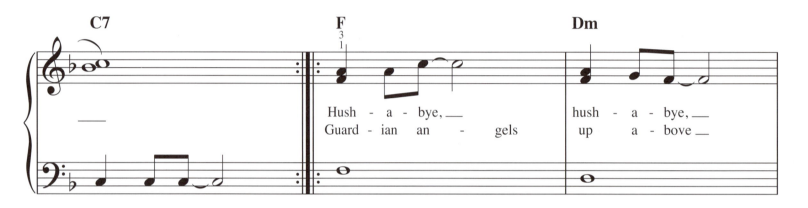

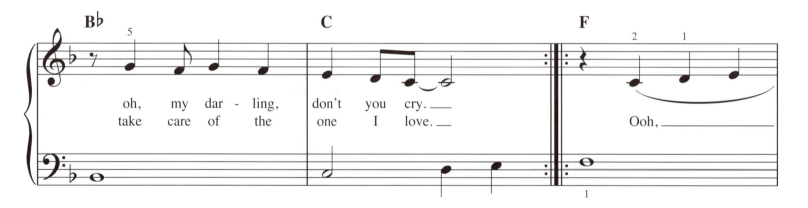

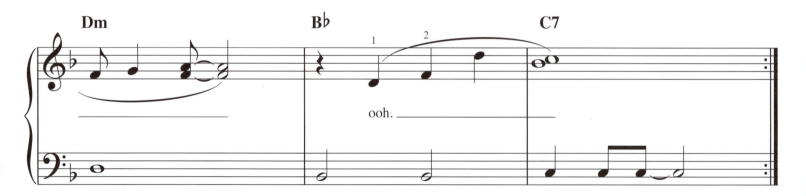

Hush - a - bye, ___ hush - a - bye, ___ oh, my dar - ling,
Guard - ian an - gels up a - bove ___ take care of the

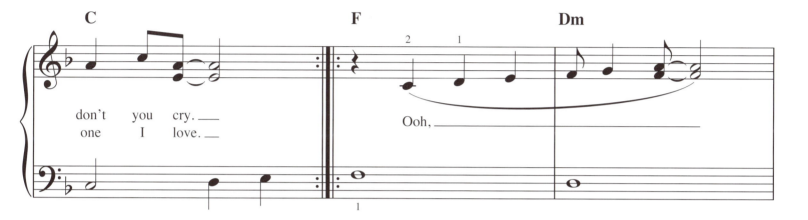

don't you cry. ___ Ooh, ___
one I love. ___

ooh. ___ Pil - lows ly - ing
Sand - man will be

on your bed; ___ oh, my dar - ling, rest your head. ___
com - ing soon, ___ sing - ing you a slum - ber tune. ___

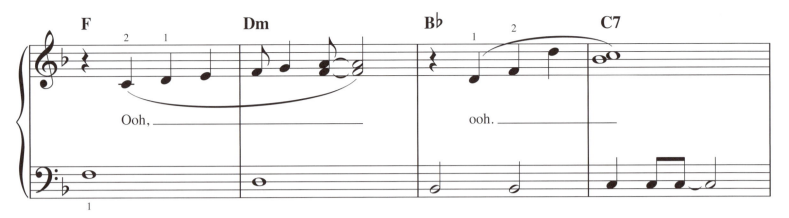

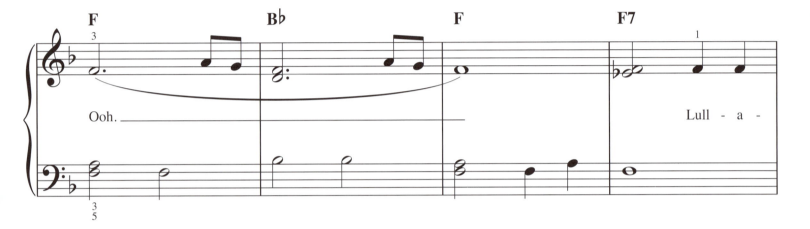

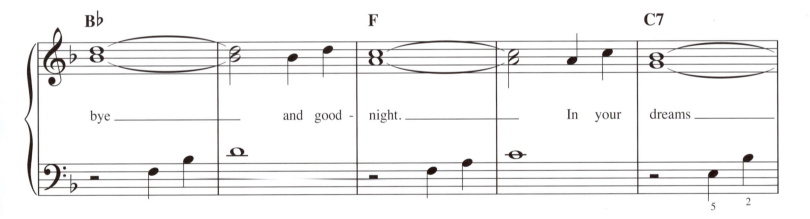

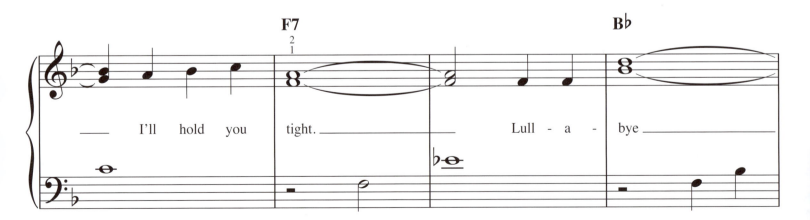

and good - night _____ till the dawn's _____ ear - ly

light. _____

Hush - a - bye, _____ hush - a - bye, _____
Guard - ian an - gels up a - bove _____

oh, my dar - ling, don't you cry. _____
take care of the one I love. _____

Ooh, _____

_____ ooh. _____

KANSAS CITY

Words and Music by JERRY LEIBER
and MIKE STOLLER

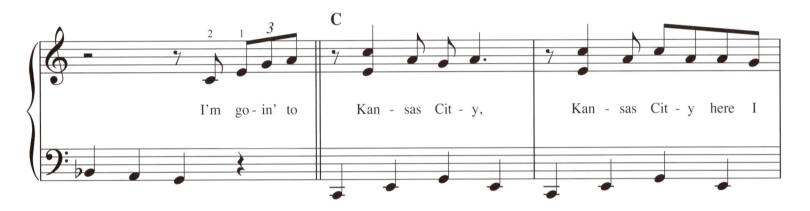

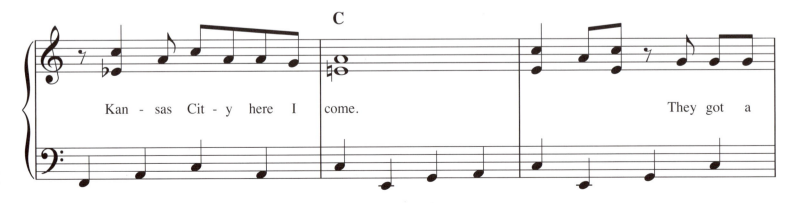

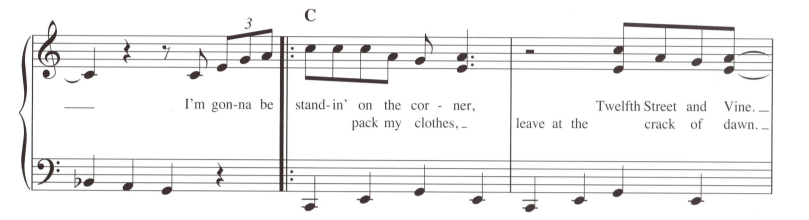

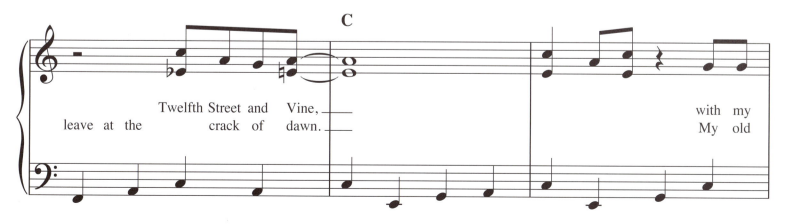

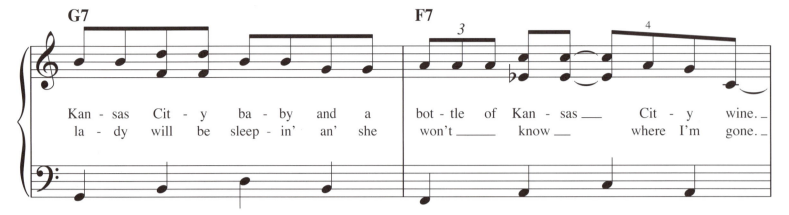

Kan - sas Cit - y ba - by and a bot - tle of Kan - sas ___ Cit - y wine. ___
la - dy will be sleep - in' an' she won't ___ know ___ where I'm gone. ___

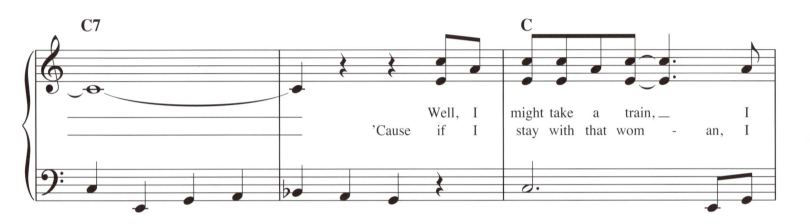

Well, I might take a train, ___ I
'Cause if I stay with that wom - an, I

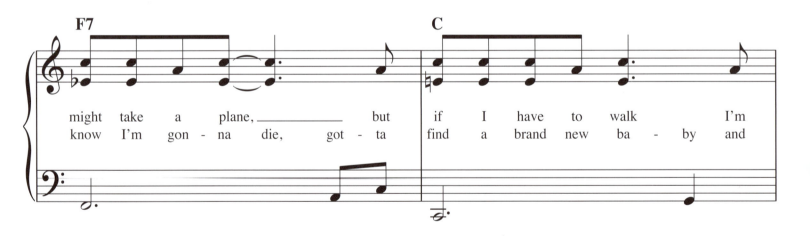

might take a plane, ___ but if I have to walk I'm
know I'm gon - na die, got - ta find a brand new ba - by and

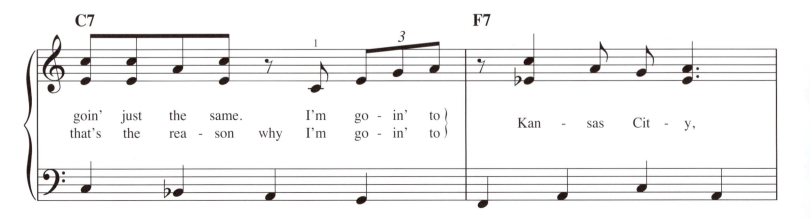

goin' just the same. I'm go - in' to
that's the rea - son why I'm go - in' to Kan - sas Cit - y,

63

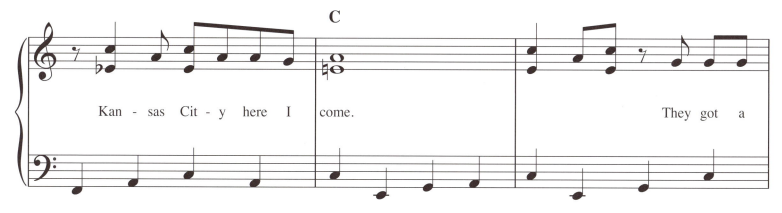

C

G7   F7   C7

cra - zy way of lov - in' there and I'm gon - na get me some.

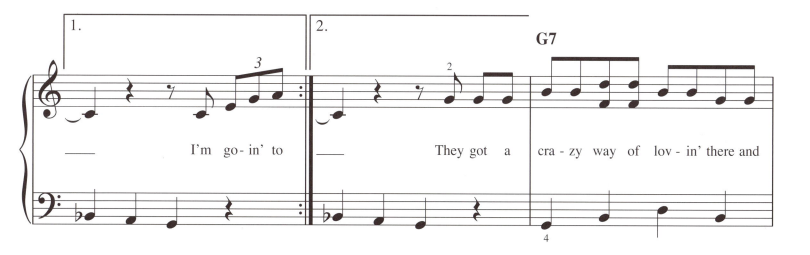

1.   2.   G7

I'm go- in' to   They got a   cra - zy way of lov - in' there and

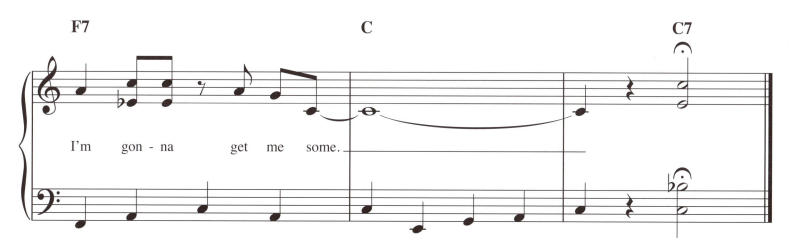

F7   C   C7

I'm gon - na get me some.

LOUIE, LOUIE

Words and Music by
RICHARD BERRY

Moderate Rock

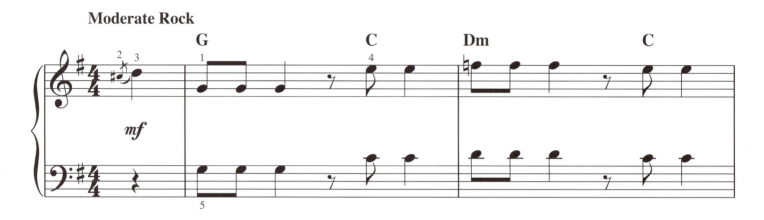

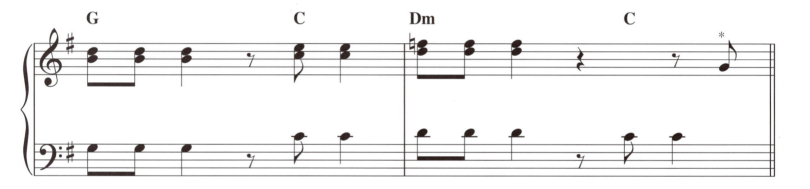

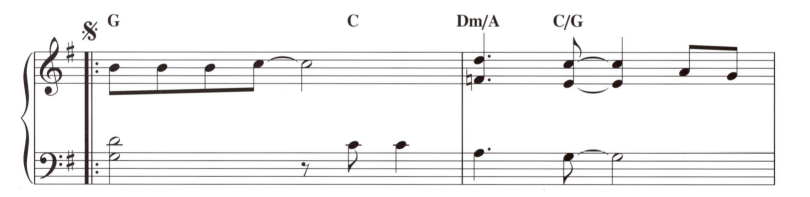

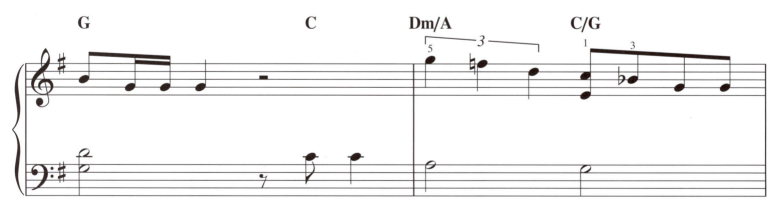

* Lyrics not printed at the request of the publisher.

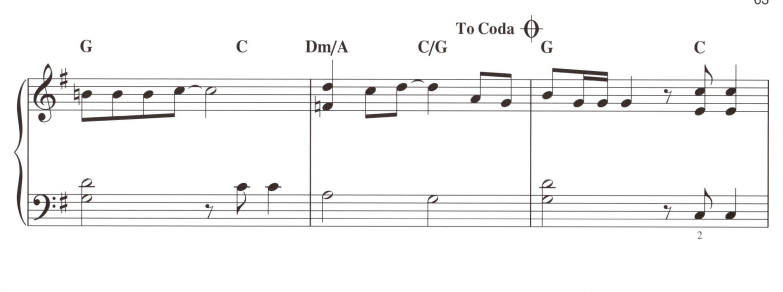

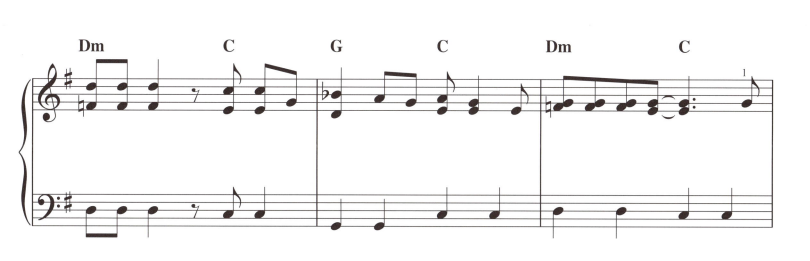

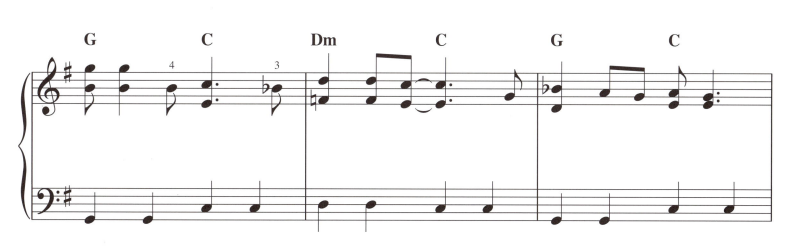

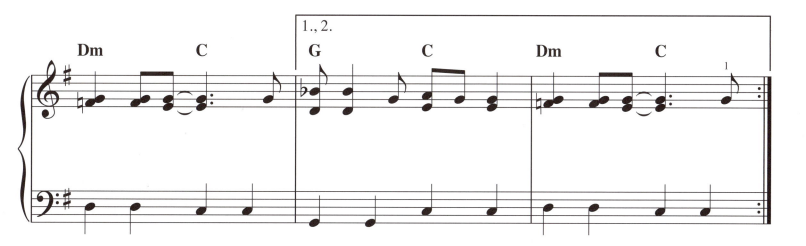

64

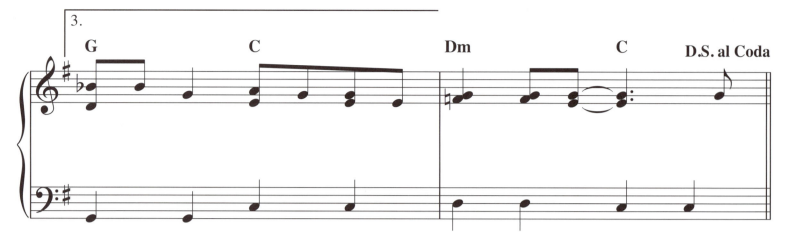

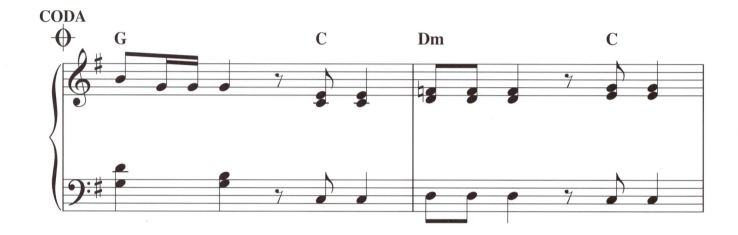

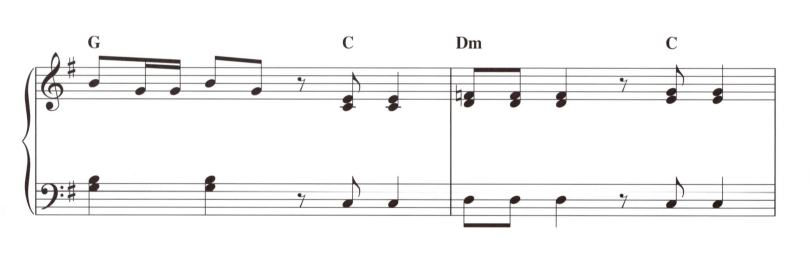

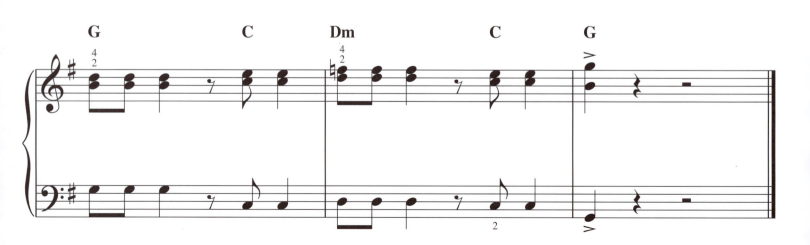

LAST KISS

Words and Music by
WAYNE COCHRAN

Moderately fast

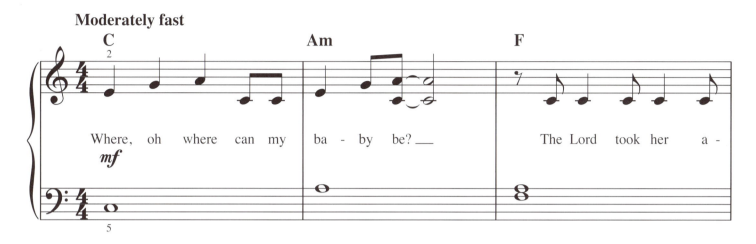

Where, oh where can my ba - by be? The Lord took her a -

way from me. She's gone to heav - en, so I got to be good so

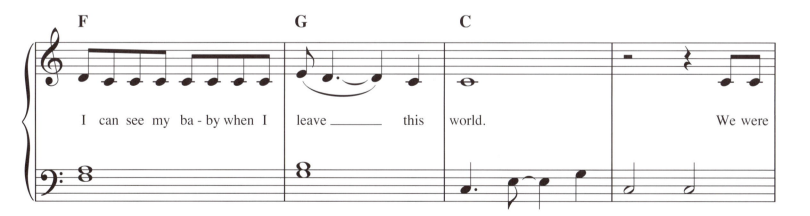

I can see my ba - by when I leave this world. We were

To Coda

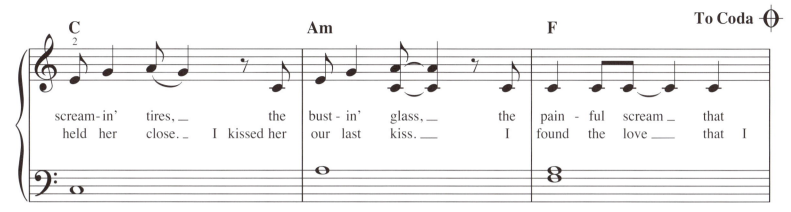

scream-in' tires, ___ the bust- in' glass, ___ the pain - ful scream ___ that
held her close. ___ I kissed her our last kiss. ___ I found the love ___ that I

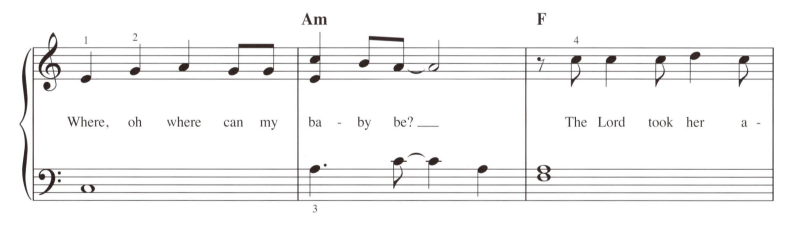

I _____ heard last. _____

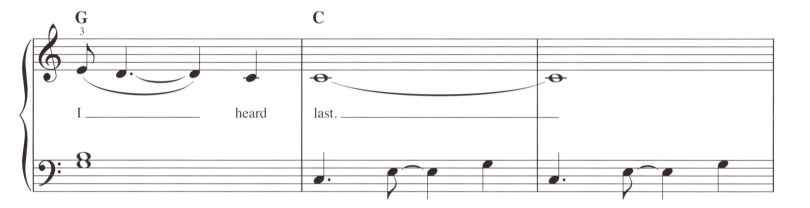

Where, oh where can my ba - by be? ___ The Lord took her a -

way from me. ___ She's gone to heav - en, so I got to be good ___ so

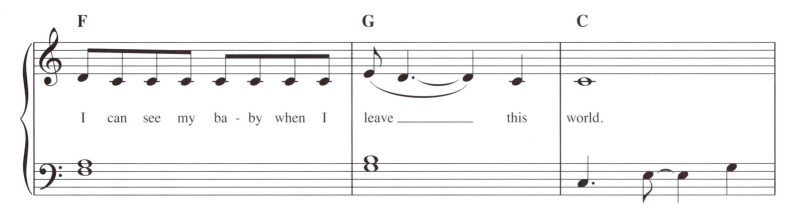

I can see my ba - by when I leave _____ this world.

D.S. al Coda

When

CODA

G

knew I would miss. ____ Well,

C

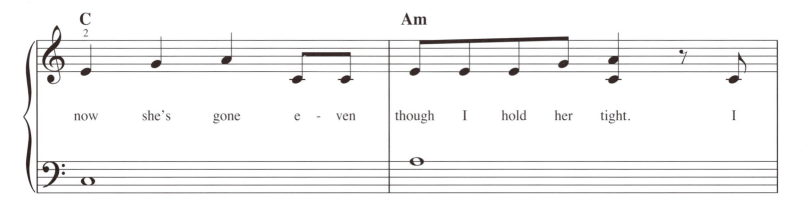

now she's gone e - ven though I hold her tight. I

Am

lost my love, my life _____ that night. _____

Where, oh where can my ba - by be? ___

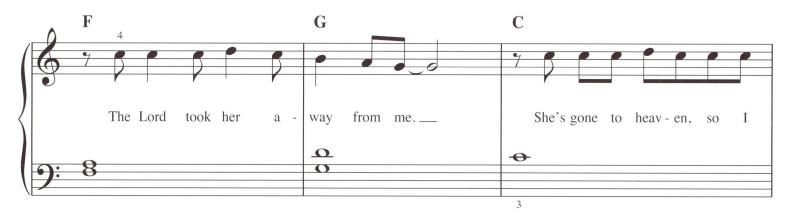

The Lord took her a - way from me. ___

She's gone to heav - en, so I

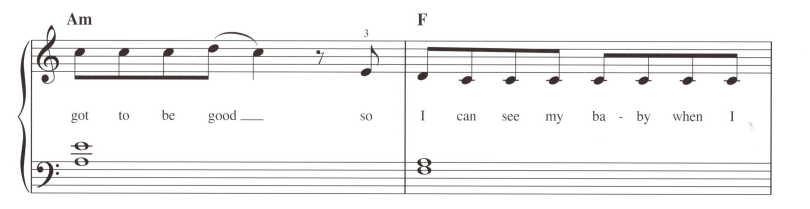

got to be good ___ so

I can see my ba - by when I

leave ___ this world. ___

THE LOCO-MOTION

Words and Music by GERRY GOFFIN
and CAROLE KING

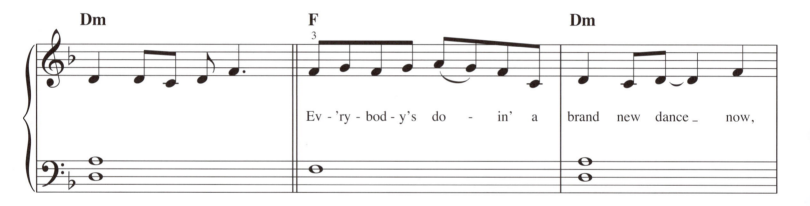

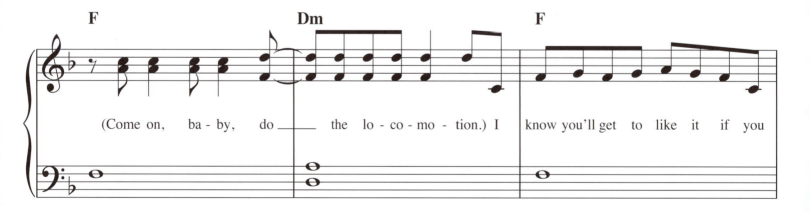

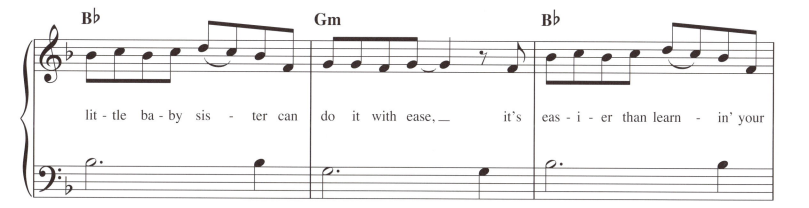

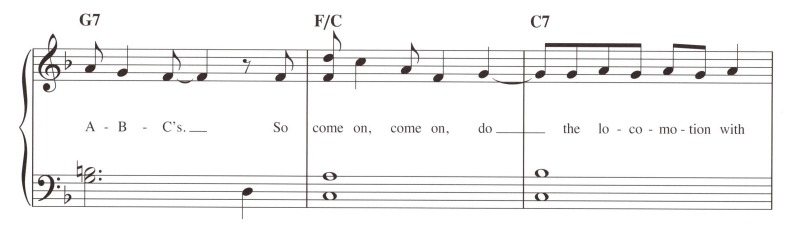

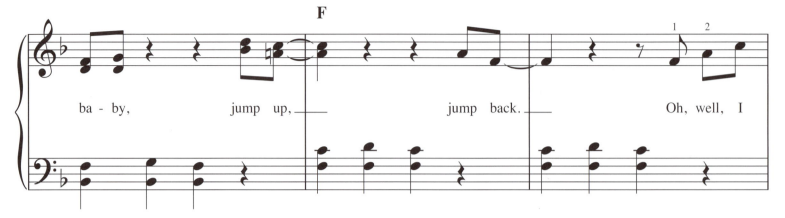

ba - by,   jump up, ____   jump back. ____   Oh, well, I

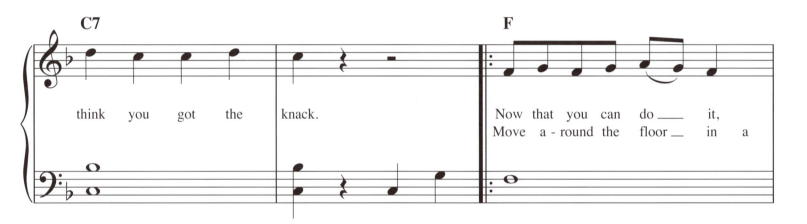

think   you   got   the   knack.   Now that you can do ____ it,
                                     Move a - round the floor ____ in a

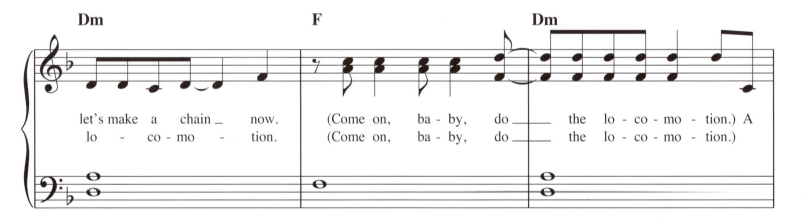

let's make a chain ____ now.   (Come on, ba - by, do ____ the lo - co - mo - tion.) A
lo - co - mo - tion.   (Come on, ba - by, do ____ the lo - co - mo - tion.)

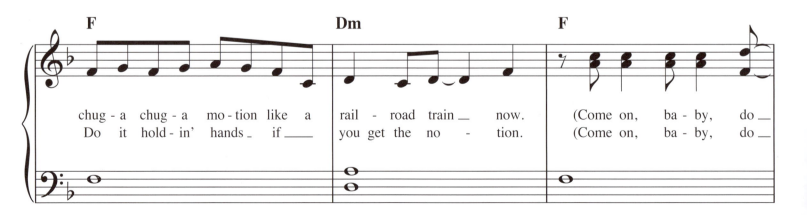

chug - a chug - a mo - tion like a   rail - road train ____ now.   (Come on, ba - by, do ____
Do it hold - in' hands ____ if ____   you get the no - tion.   (Come on, ba - by, do ____

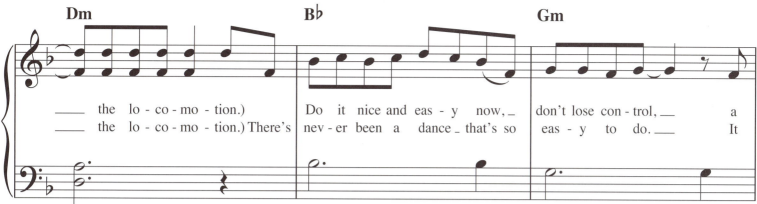

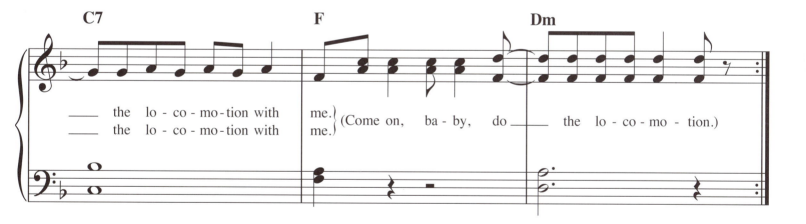

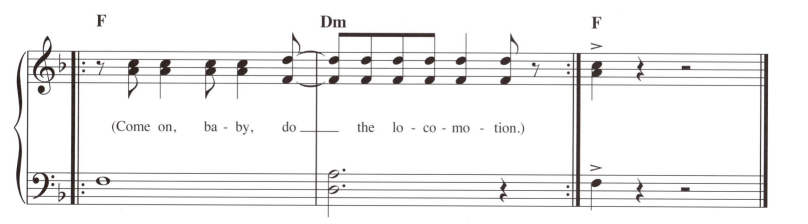

LONELY BOY

Words and Music by
PAUL ANKA

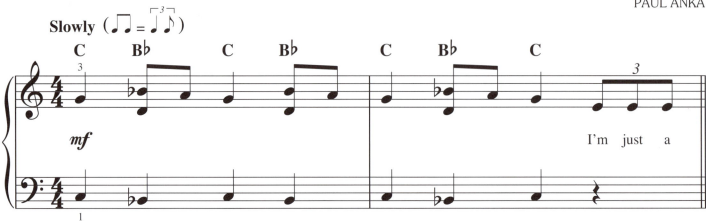

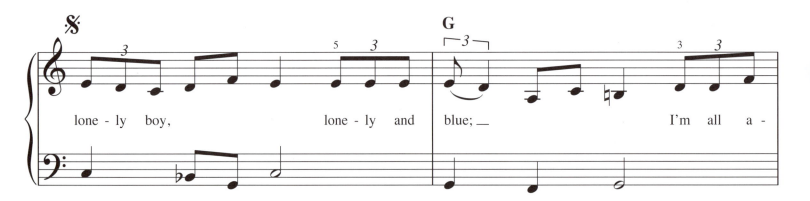

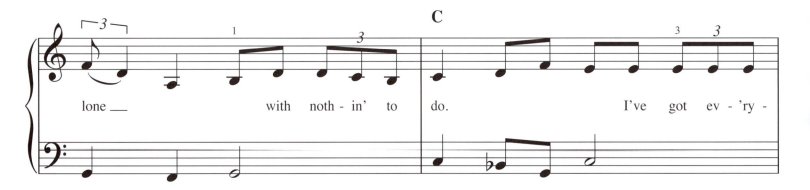

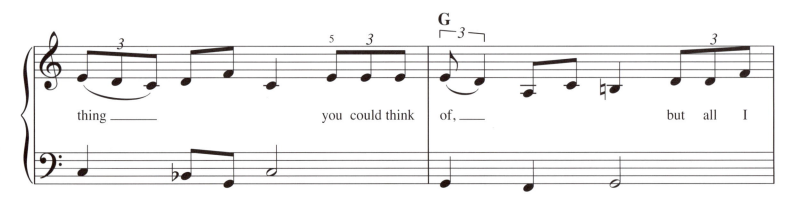

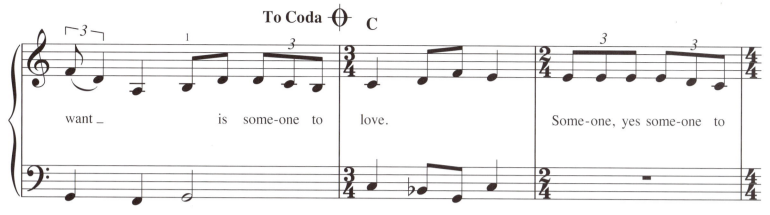

D.S. al Coda

love _   each night and   day.   I'm just a

CODA

love.   Some-bod - y, some-bod - y, some-bod - y,   please _   send her to

me. _   I'll make her hap-py,   just wait and   see.   I've prayed so

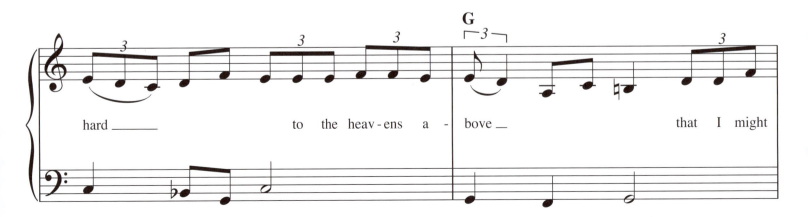

hard _____   to the heav-ens a - bove _   that I might

find _ some-one to love. I'm just a lone-ly boy, lone-ly and

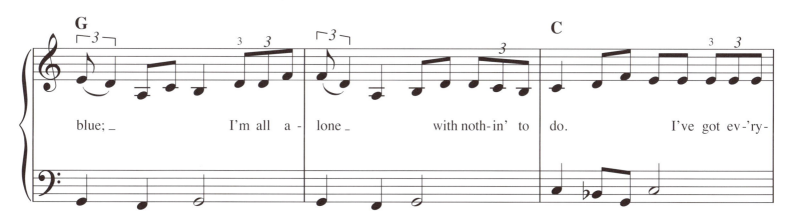

blue; _ I'm all a - lone _ with noth-in' to do. I've got ev-'ry-

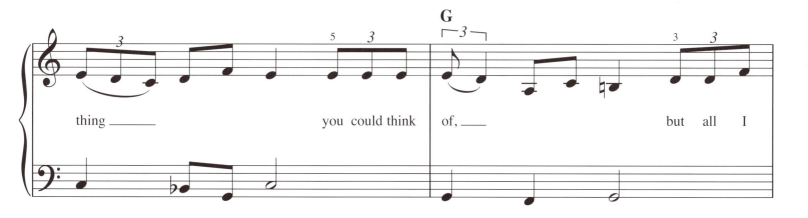

thing _____ you could think of, ____ but all I

want _ is some-one to love.

MY SPECIAL ANGEL

Words and Music by
JIMMY DUNCAN

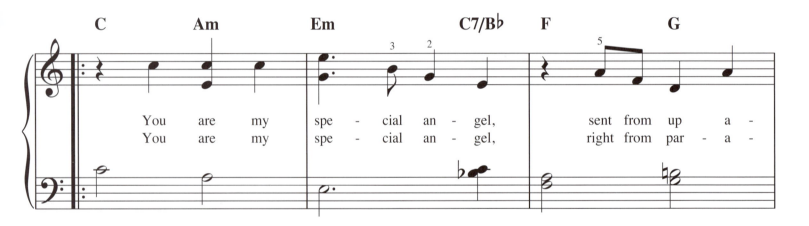

You are my spe - cial an - gel, sent from up a -
You are my spe - cial an - gel, right from par - a -

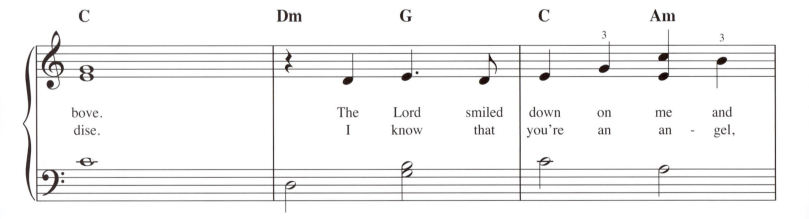

bove.
dise.
The Lord smiled down on me and
I know that you're an an - gel,

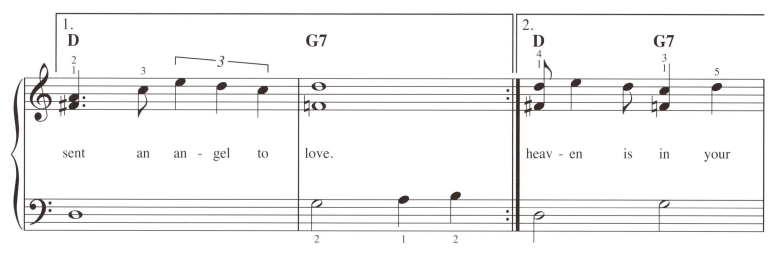

sent an an - gel to love. heav - en is in your

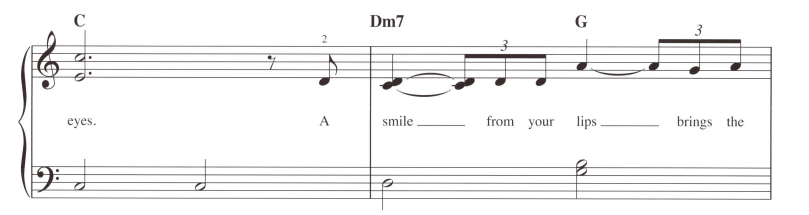

eyes. A smile _____ from your lips _____ brings the

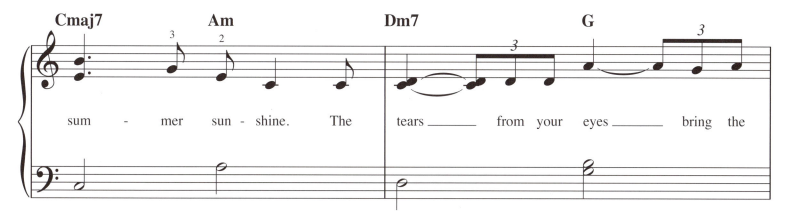

sum - mer sun - shine. The tears _____ from your eyes _____ bring the

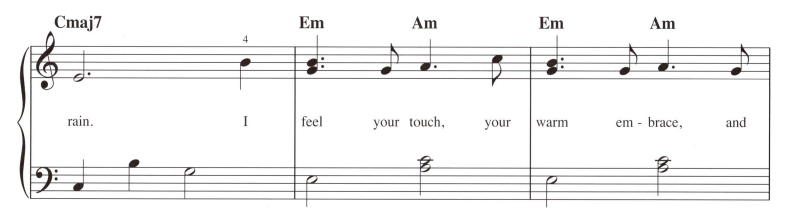

rain. I feel your touch, your warm em - brace, and

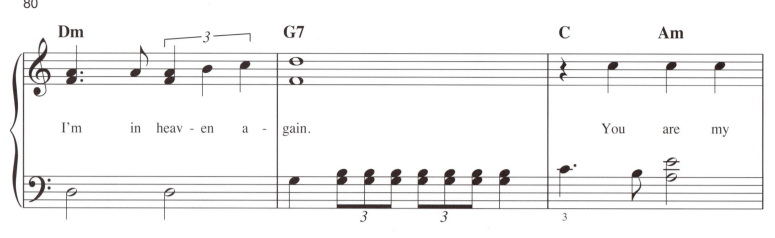

I'm in heav - en a - gain.   You are my

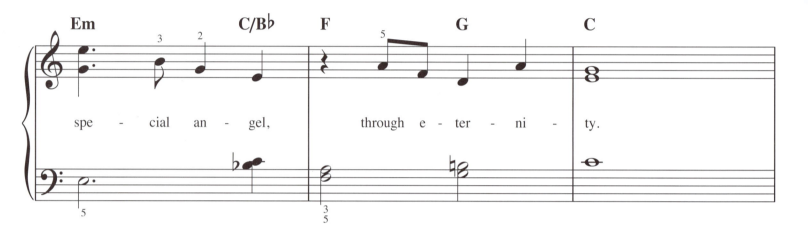

spe - cial an - gel,   through e - ter - ni - ty.

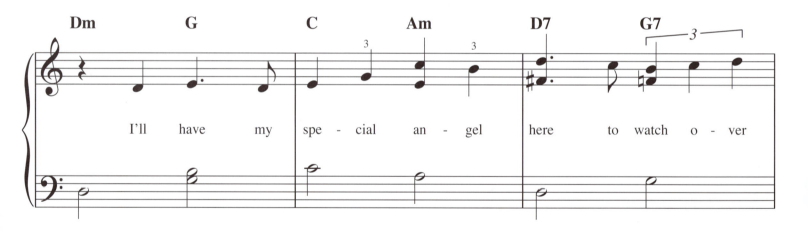

I'll have my spe - cial an - gel   here   to watch o - ver

me.

PRIMROSE LANE

Words and Music by WAYNE SHANKLIN
and GEORGE CALLENDER

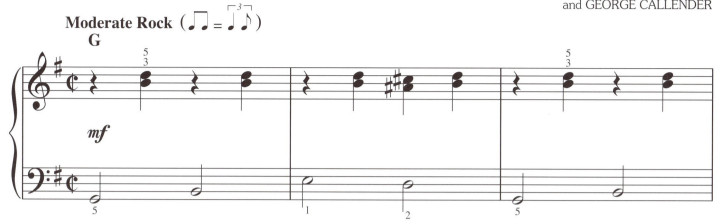

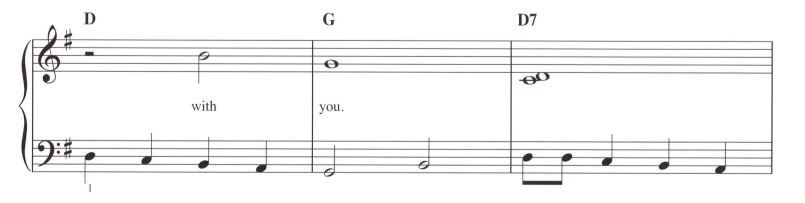

Can't ex - plain, __ when we're walk - in' down the Prim - rose Lane, __

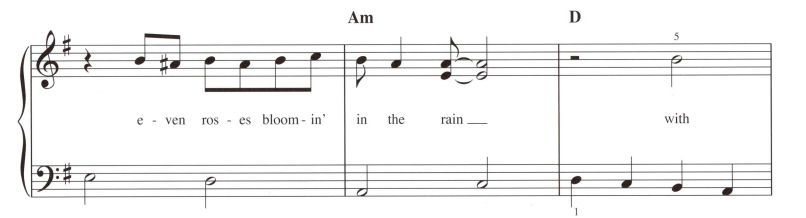

e - ven ros - es bloom - in' in the rain __ with

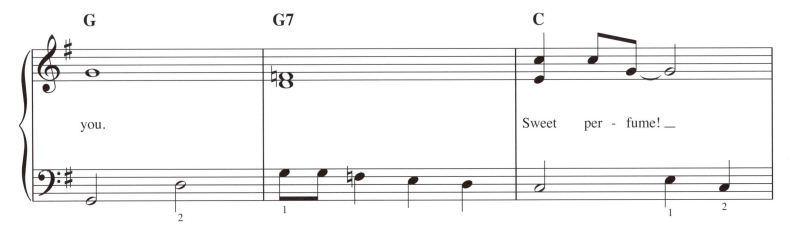

you. Sweet per - fume! __

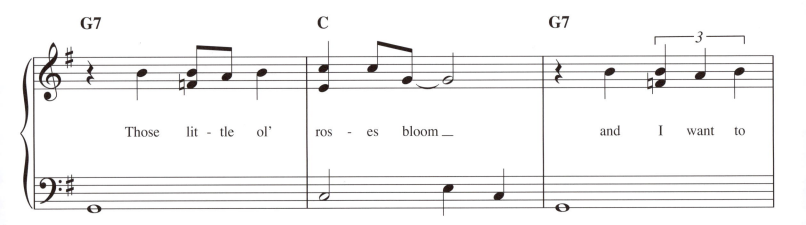

Those lit - tle ol' ros - es bloom __ and I want to

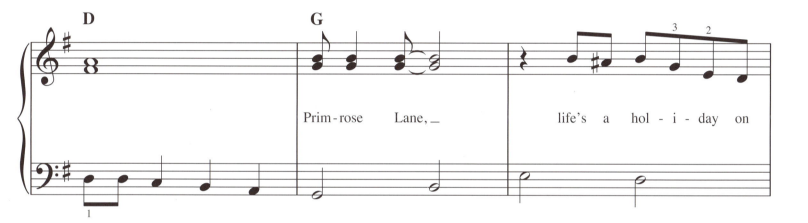

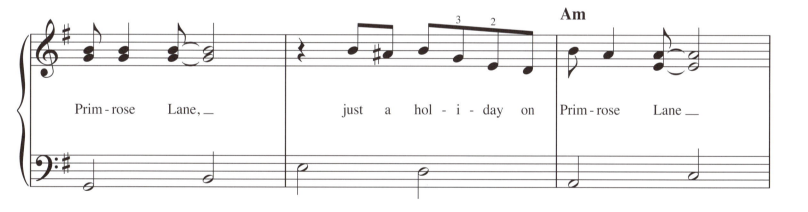

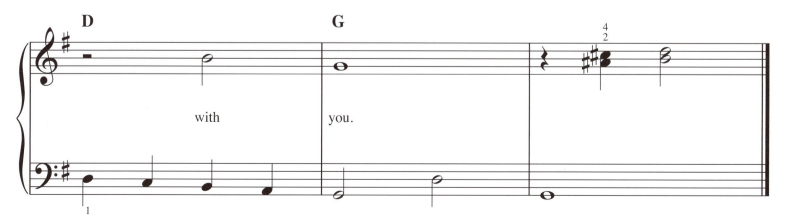

NO PARTICULAR PLACE TO GO

Words and Music by
CHUCK BERRY

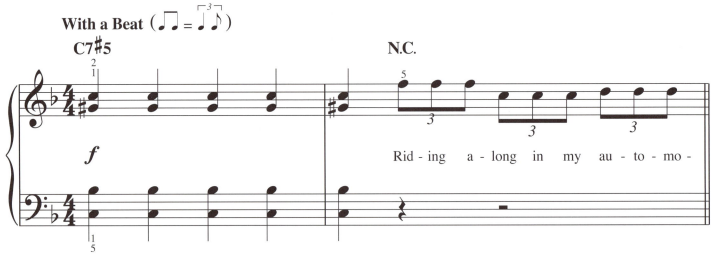

Riding along in my auto-mo-

bile,
bile,
go,
boose,

my baby beside me at the
I was an-xious to tell her the way I
so we parked way out on the co-ca-
still try-ing to get her belt un-

wheel,
feel.
mo.
loose.

I stole a kiss at the turn of a
So I told her soft-ly and sin-ly
The night was young and the moon was
All the way home I held a

Bb7

mile,
cere,
gold,
grudge,

my cu - ri - os - i - ty run - ning
and she leaned and whis - pered in my
so we both de - cid - ed to take a
for the safe - ty belt ___ that would - n't

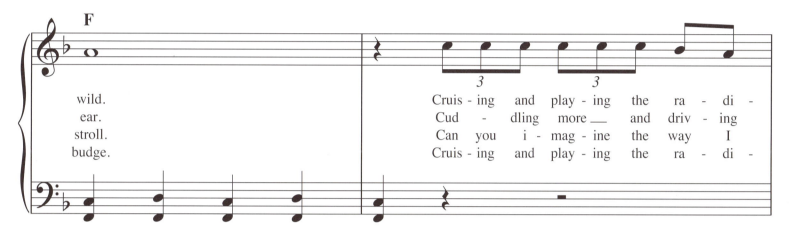

F

wild.
ear.
stroll.
budge.

Cruis - ing and play - ing the ra - di -
Cud - dling more ___ and driv - ing
Can you i - mag - ine the way I
Cruis - ing and play - ing the ra - di -

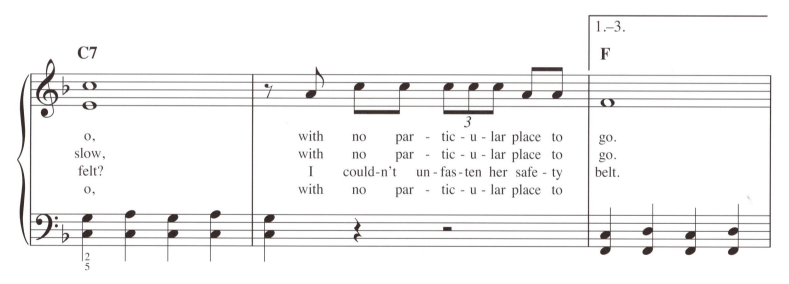

C7

1.–3.

F

o,
slow,
felt?
o,

with no par - tic - u - lar place to go.
with no par - tic - u - lar place to go.
I could - n't un - fas - ten her safe - ty belt.
with no par - tic - u - lar place to

N.C.

4.

F7   **Bb Db7/B   C   F**

Rid - ing a - long in my au - to - mo - go.
No ___ par - tic - u - lar place to
Rid - ing a - long in my cal - a -

OH, PRETTY WOMAN

Words and Music by ROY ORBISON
and BILL DEES

Moderate Rock

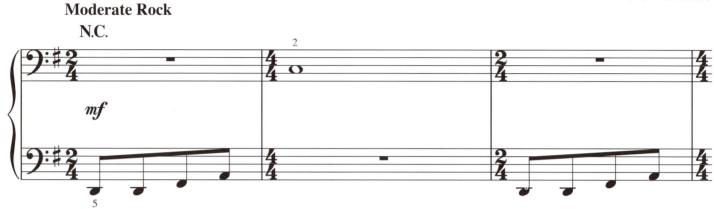

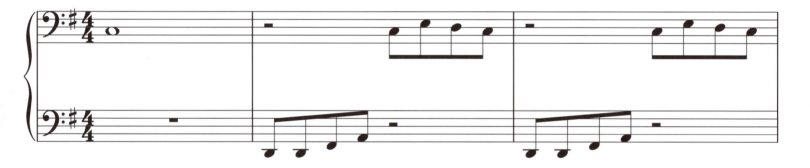

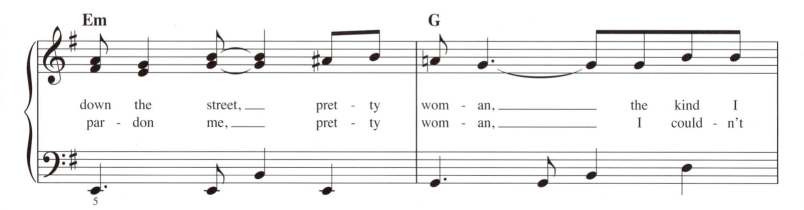

Pret - ty wom - an, _____ walk - ing
wom - an, _____ won't you

down the street, ___ pret - ty wom - an, _____ the kind I
par - don me, ___ pret - ty wom - an, _____ I could - n't

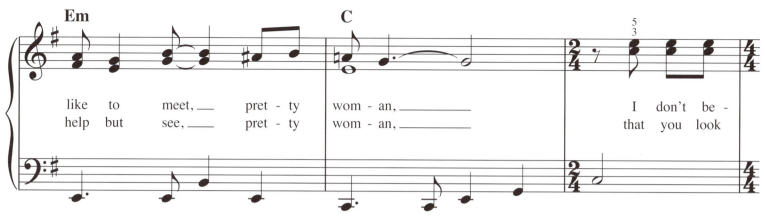

like to meet, ___ pret - ty wom - an, ____ I don't be -
help but see, ___ pret - ty wom - an, ____ that you look

lieve you, _____ you're not the truth; _____ no one could
love - ly _____ as can be; _____ are you

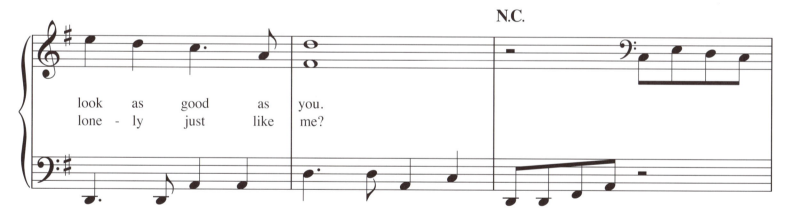

look as good as you.
lone - ly just like me?

Pret - ty

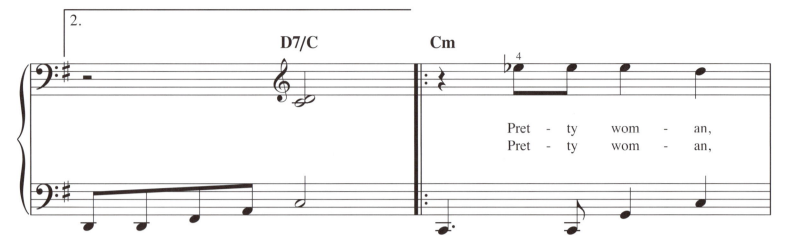

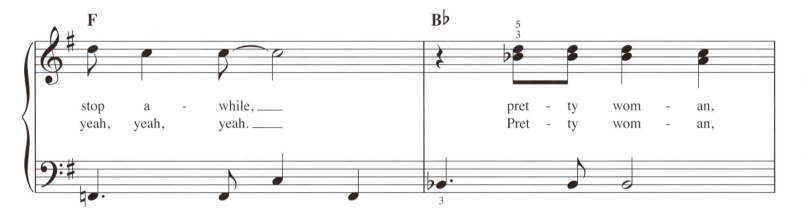

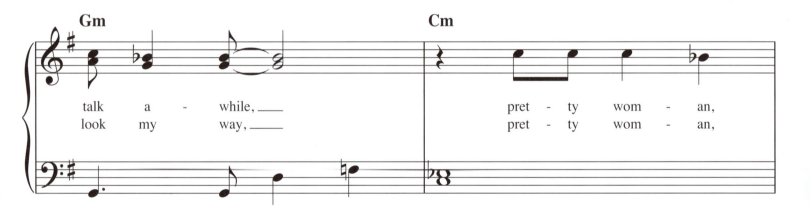

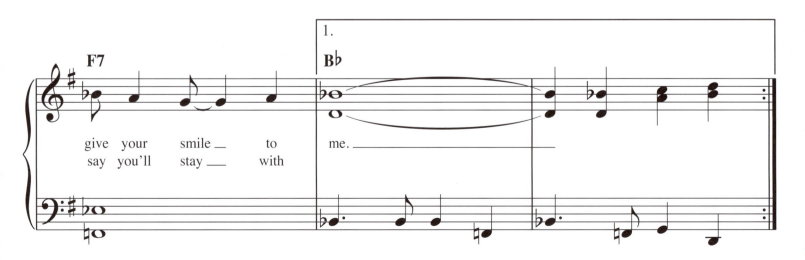

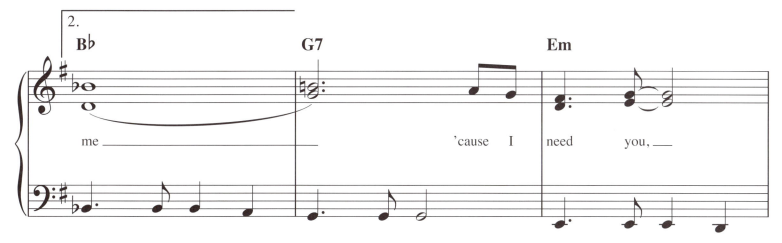

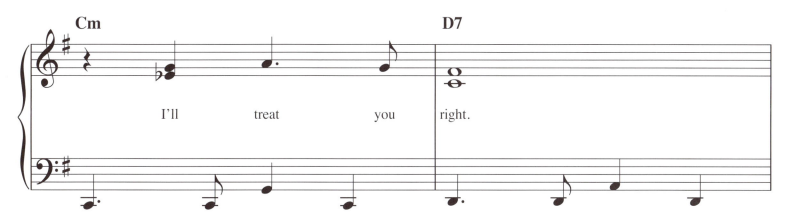

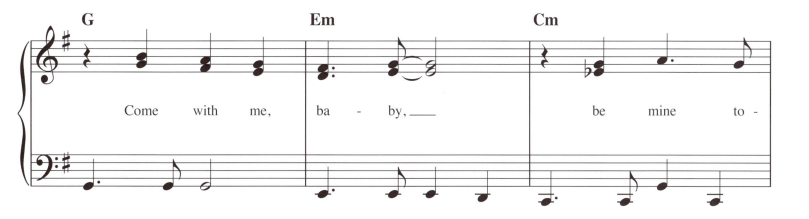

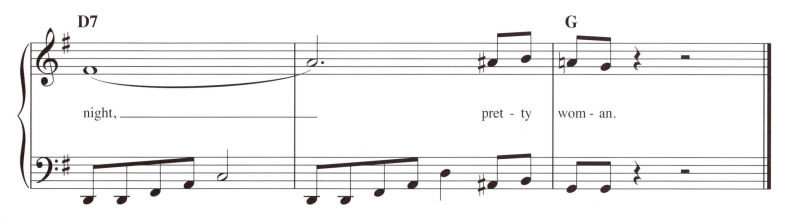

ROCK AROUND THE CLOCK

Words and Music by MAX C. FREEDMAN
and JIMMY DeKNIGHT

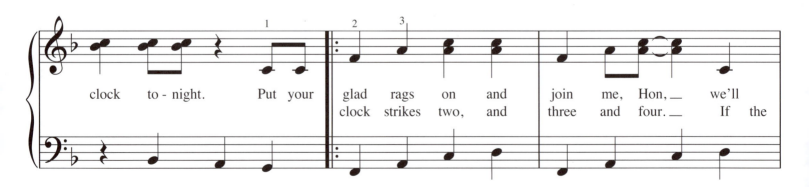

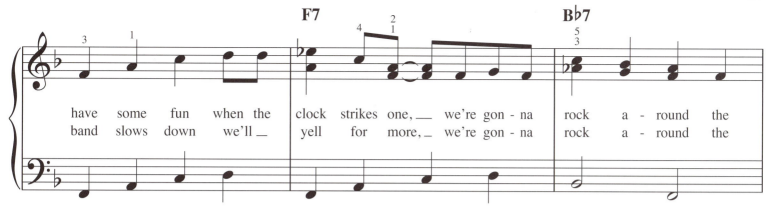

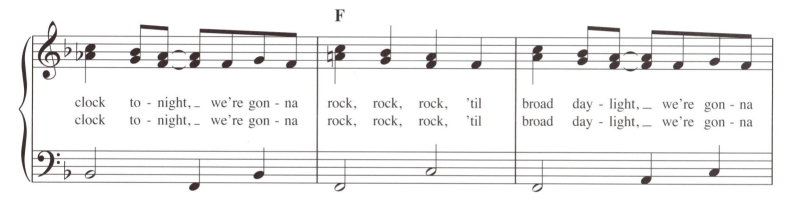

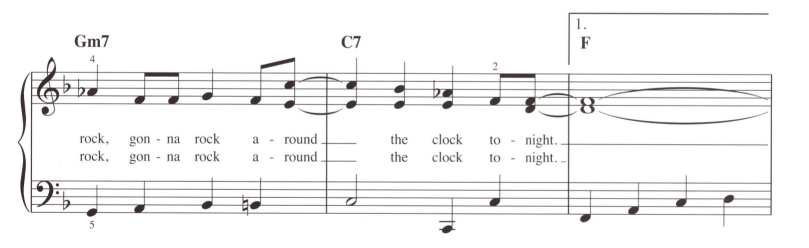

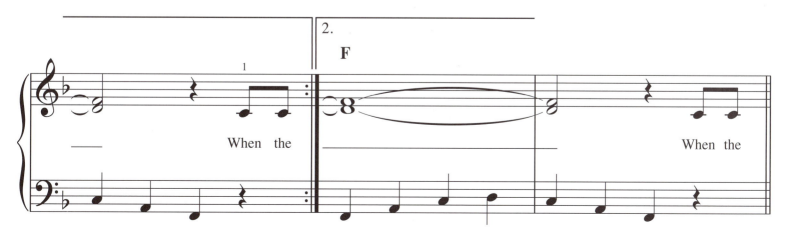

chimes ring five and six and seven,_ we'll be rock - in' up in
eight, nine, ten, e - lev - en, too, ___ I'll be go - in' strong and
clock strikes twelve, we'll cool off, then, ___ start a rock - in' 'round the

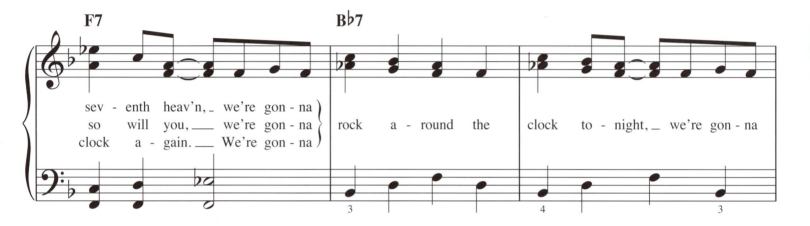

F7 **B♭7**

sev - enth heav'n,_ we're gon - na ⎫
so will you, ___ we're gon - na ⎬ rock a - round the clock to - night,_ we're gon - na
clock a - gain. ___ We're gon - na ⎭

F **Gm7** **C**

rock, rock, rock, 'til broad day - light,_we're gon - na rock, gon-na rock a - round ___ the clock to - night._

1., 2. **3.**
F **F** **B♭7** **F** **F9**

When it's
When the

ROCKET 88

Words and Music by
JACKIE BRENSTON

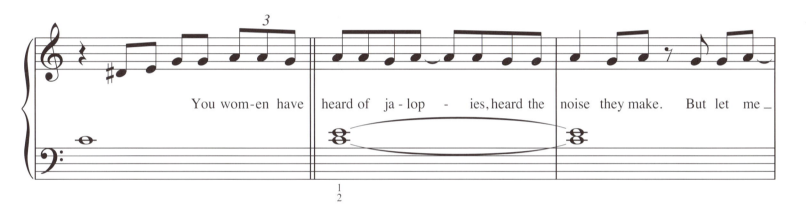

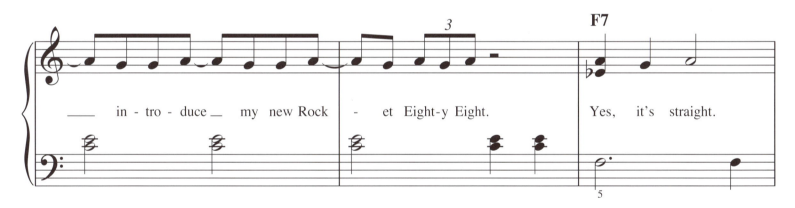

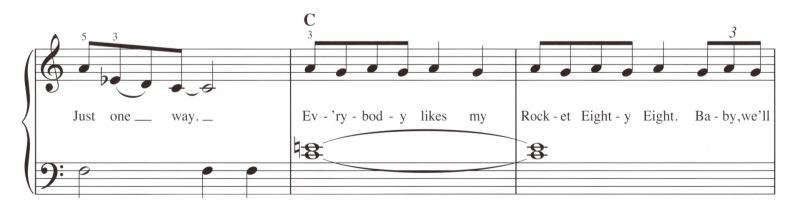

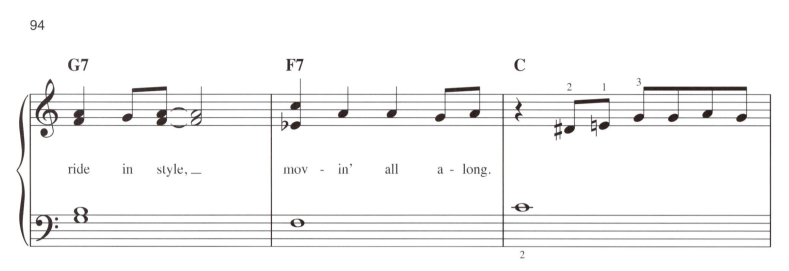

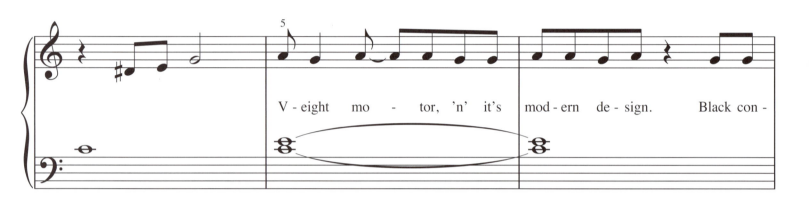

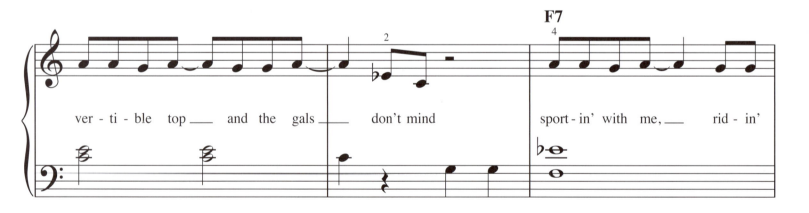

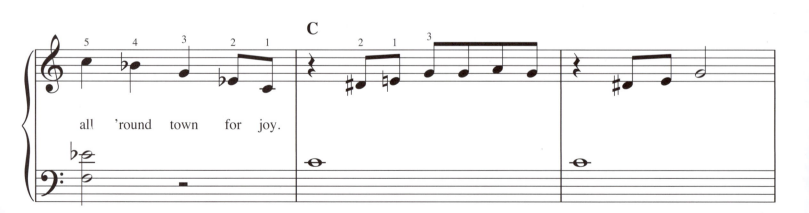

Step in my Rock - et and don't be late. Ba - by we're ___ pull - ing out ___ a - bout

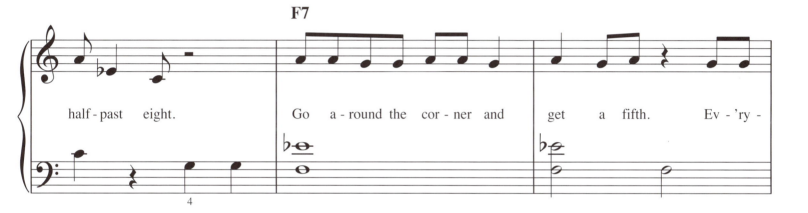

F7

half - past eight. Go a - round the cor - ner and get a fifth. Ev - 'ry -

C   **G7**

one in my car's ___ gon - na take a lit - tle nip. Move on out, ooz -

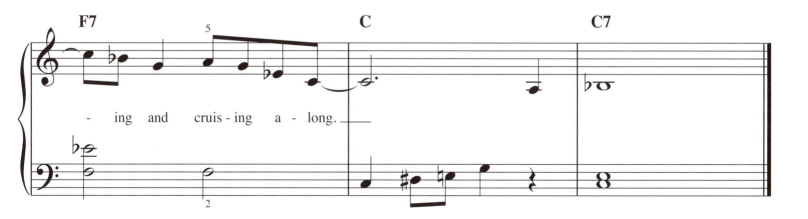

F7   **C**   **C7**

- ing and cruis - ing a - long. ___

ROCKIN' ROBIN

Words and Music by
J. THOMAS

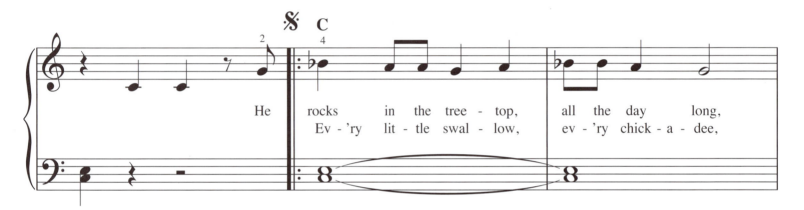

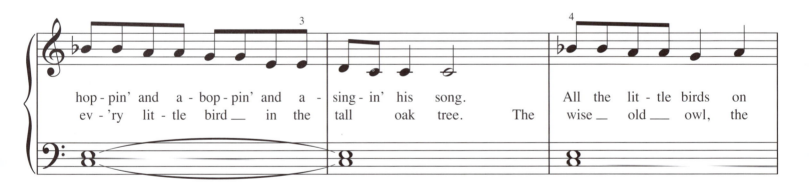

Rob - in, Rock - in' Rob - in.

Blow, Rock - in' Rob - in, 'cause we're real - ly gon - na rock to - night.

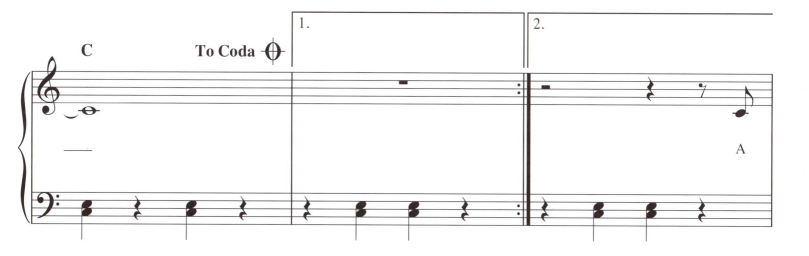

To Coda ⊕

1.

2.

A

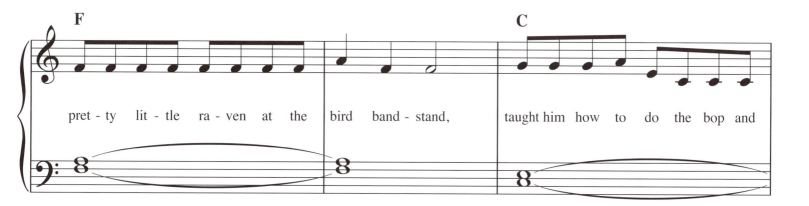

pret - ty lit - tle ra - ven at the bird band - stand, taught him how to do the bop and

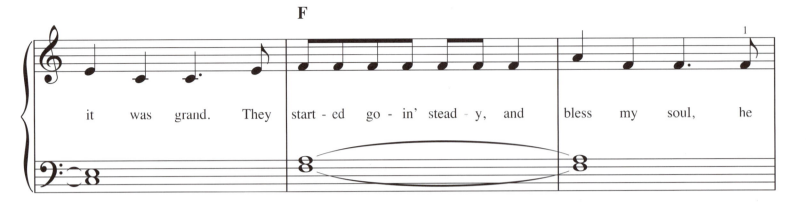

it was grand. They start-ed go-in' stead-y, and bless my soul, he

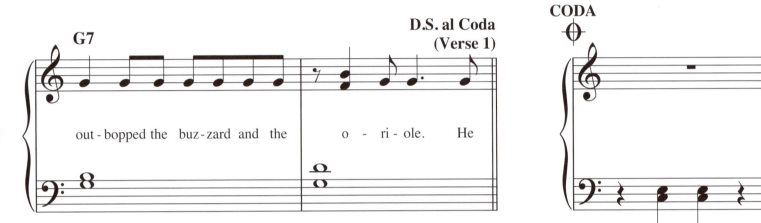

out-bopped the buz-zard and the o - ri-ole. He

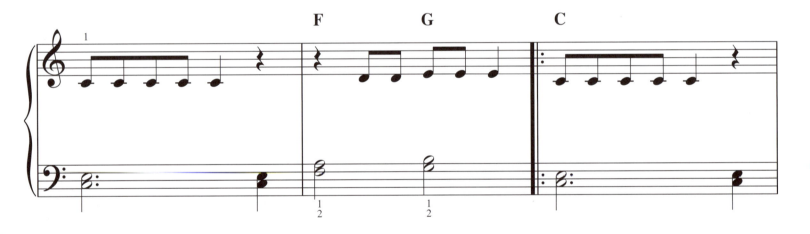

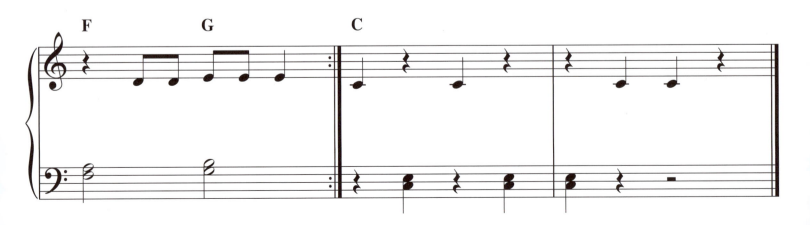

RUNAROUND SUE

Words and Music by ERNIE MARASCA
and DION DI MUCCI

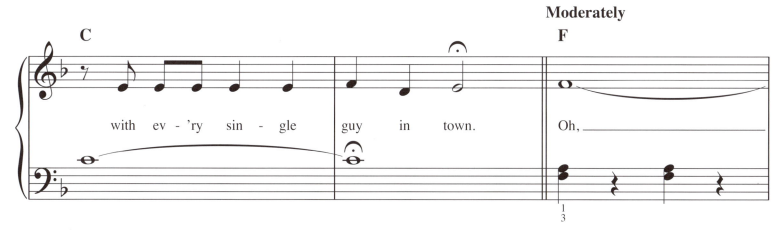

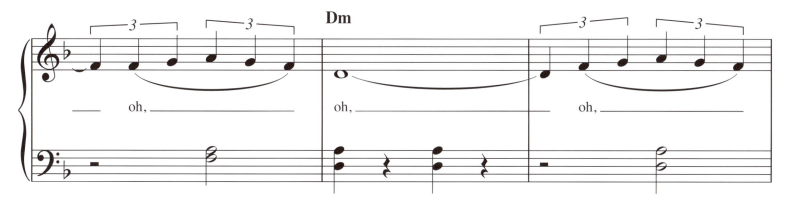

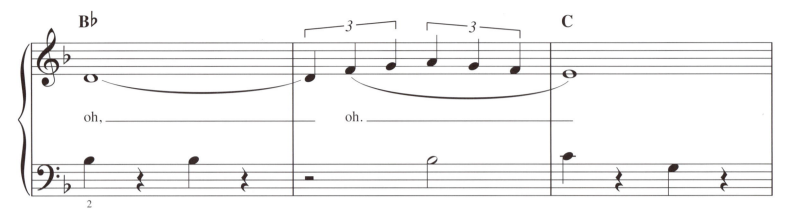

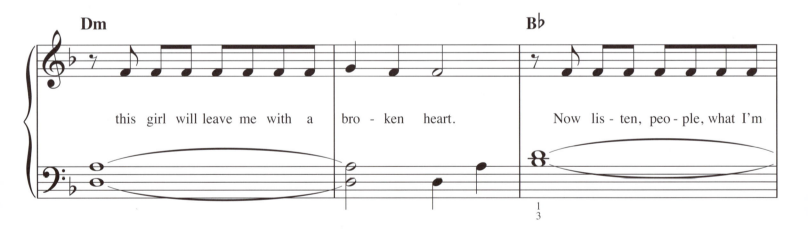

I miss her lips and the smile on her face, __ the touch of her hair __ and this

girl's warm em - brace. __ So if you don't wan - na cry like I do, __

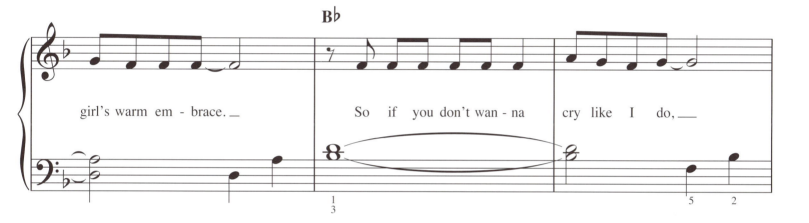

a - keep a - way from a Run - a - round Sue. Oh, _____

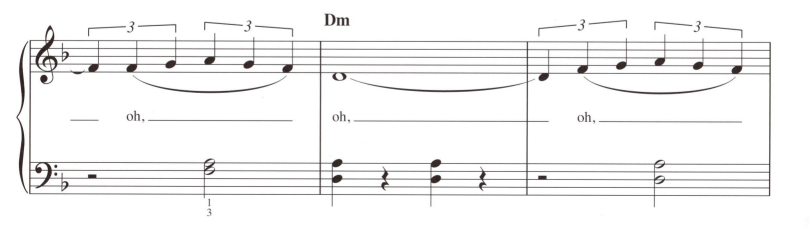

__ oh, _____ oh, _____ oh, _____

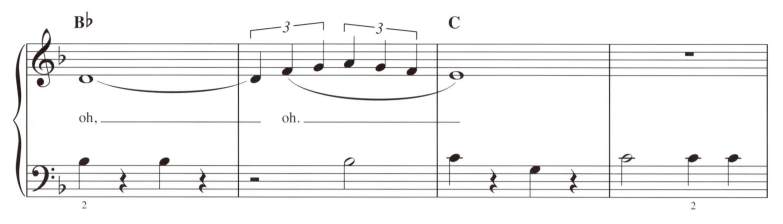

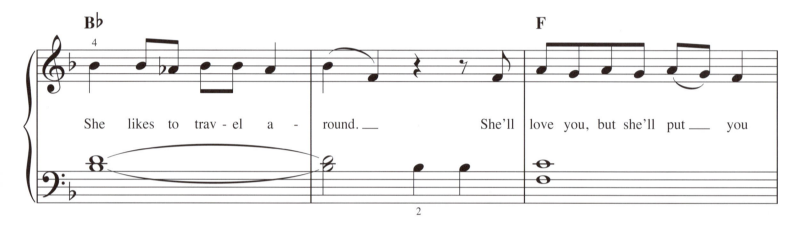

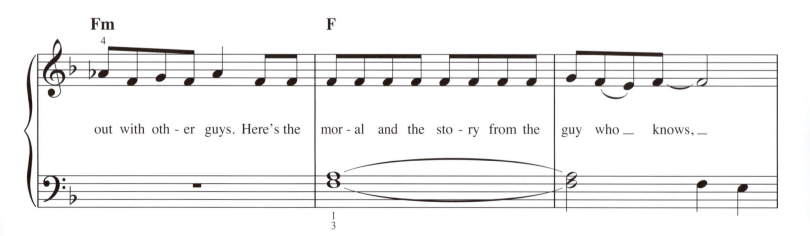

I fell in love and my love __ still __ grows. __ Ask an - y fool that

she ev - er knew, __ they'll say keep a - way from - a Run - a - round Sue.

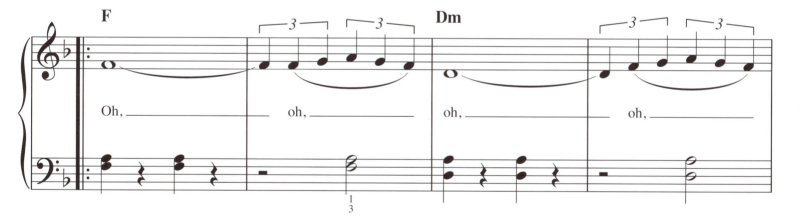

Oh, _____ oh, _____ oh, _____ oh,

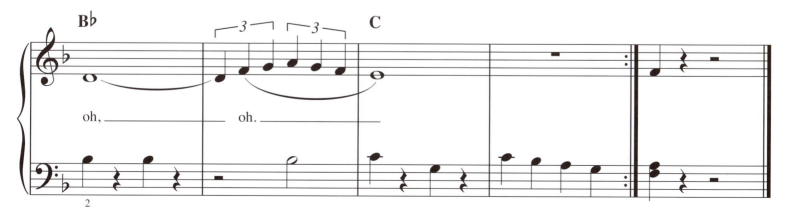

oh, _____ oh. _____

RUNAWAY

Words and Music by MAX CROOK
and DEL SHANNON

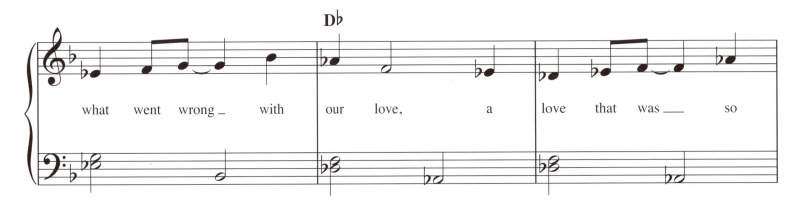

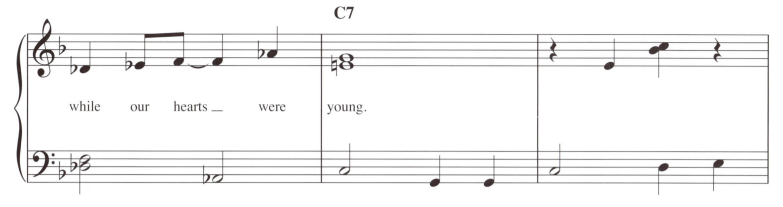

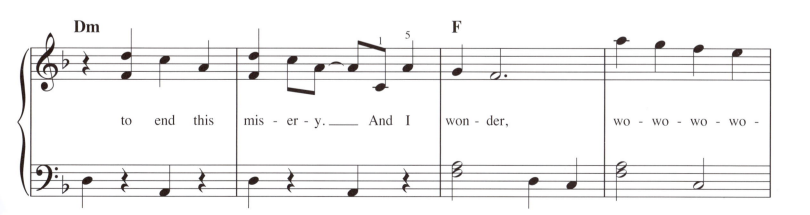

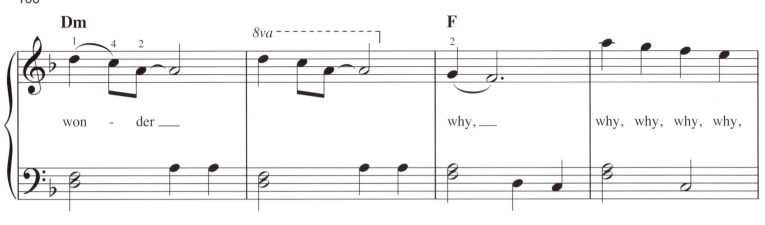

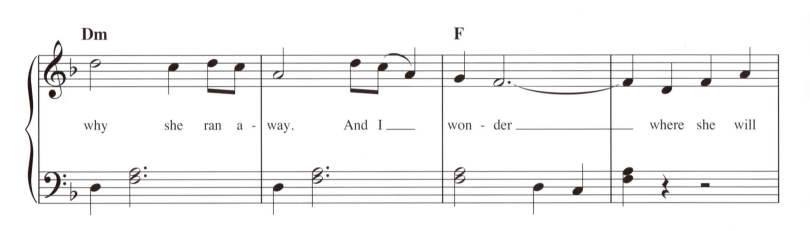

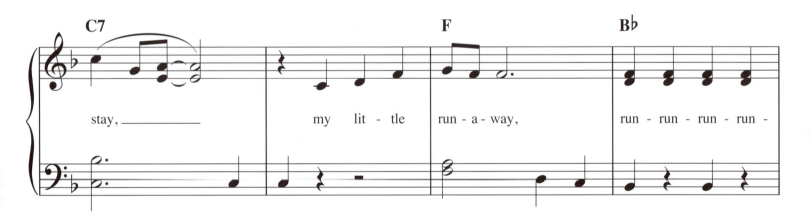

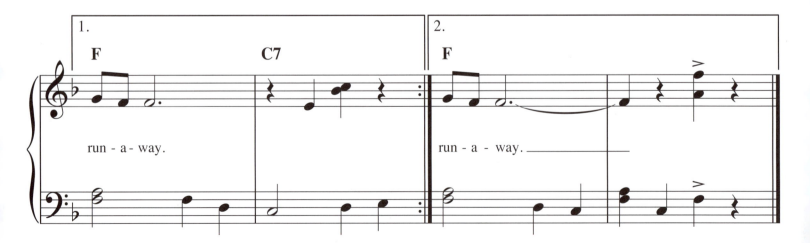

Secretly

Words and Music by AL HOFFMAN,
DICK MANNING and MARK MARKWELL

Moderately slow Swing

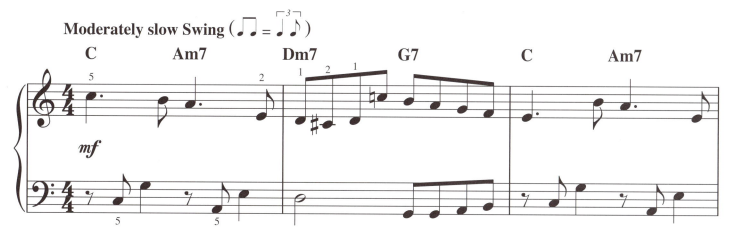

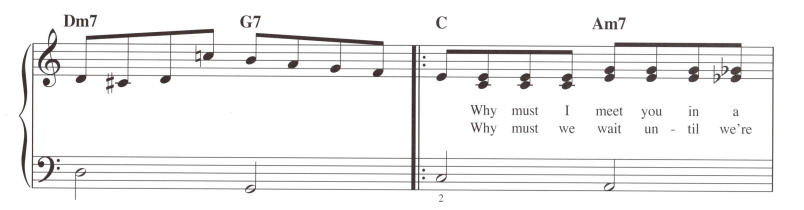

Why must I meet you in a
Why must we wait un-til we're

se-cret ren-de-vouz?
danc-ing cheek to cheek

Why must we steal a-way to
to whis-per all the words of

steal a kiss or two?
love we long to speak?

Why must we wait to do the
Why must our love be like a

108

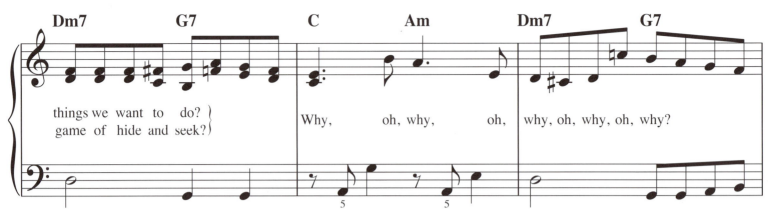

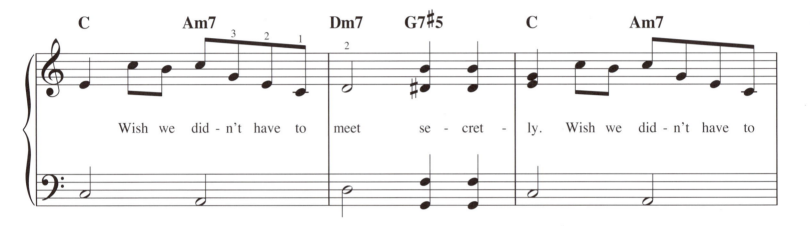

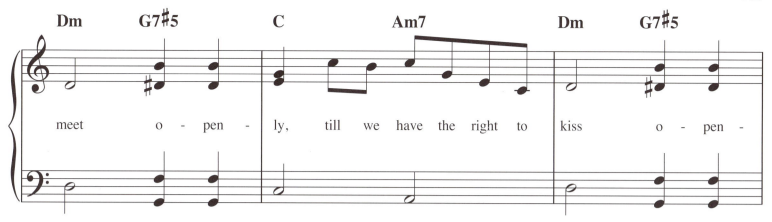

meet o - pen - ly, till we have the right to kiss o - pen -

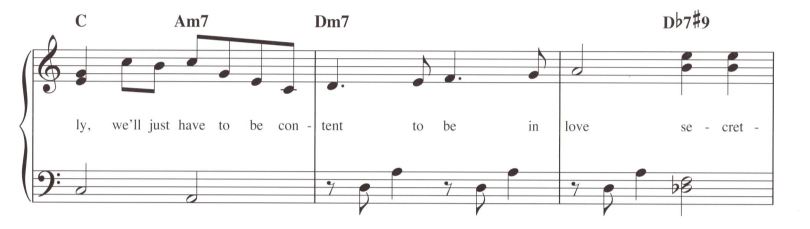

ly, we'll just have to be con - tent to be in love se - cret -

ly!

ly!

SEA OF LOVE

Words and Music by GEORGE KHOURY
and PHILIP BAPTISTE

With a slow Rock beat

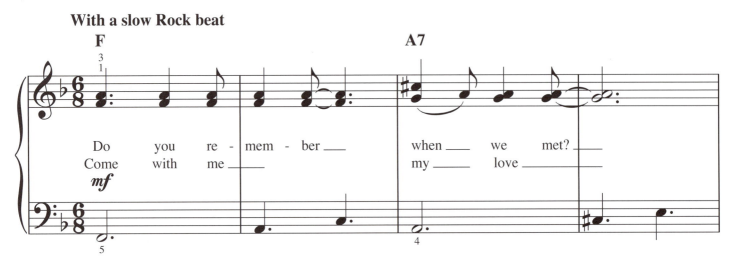

Do you re-mem-ber ___ when ___ we met?
Come with me ___ my ___ love ___

That's the day ___ I
to the sea, ___ the

knew you were my ___ pet.
sea ___ of ___ love.

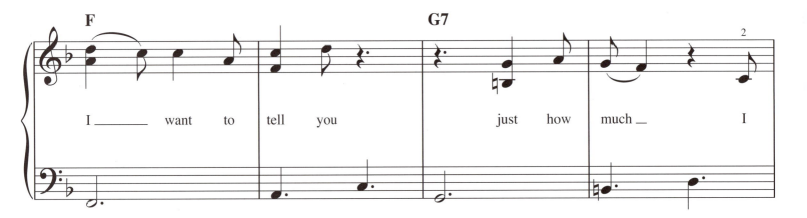

I ___ want to tell you just how much ___ I

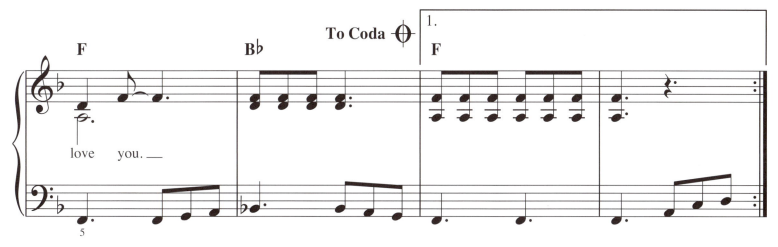

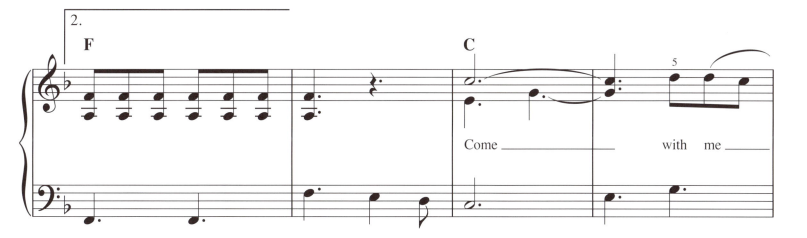

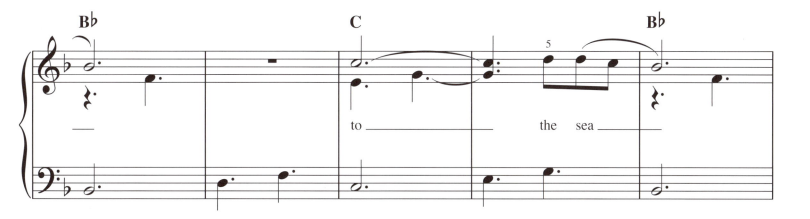

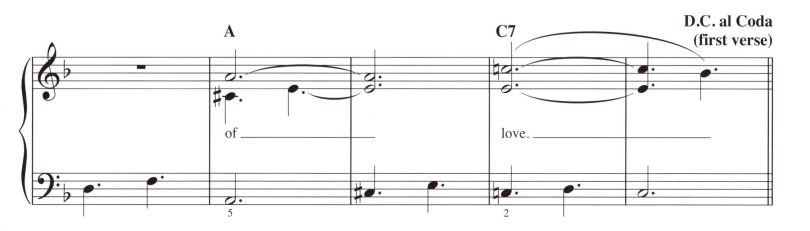

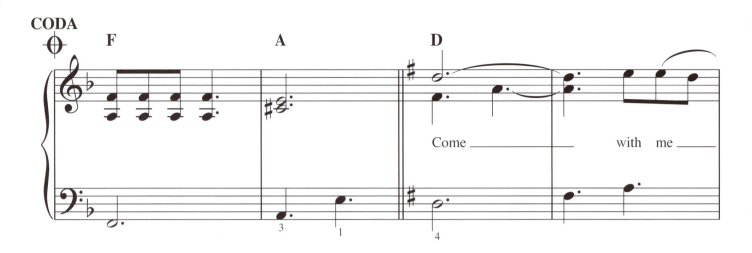

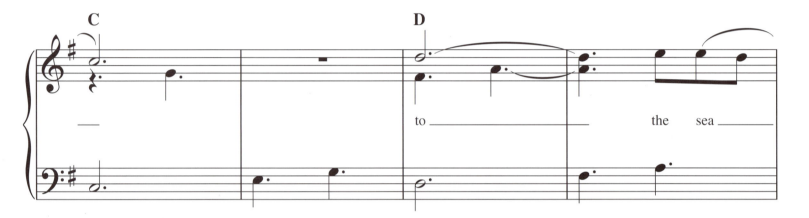

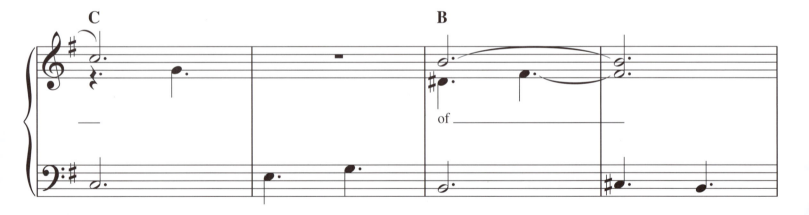

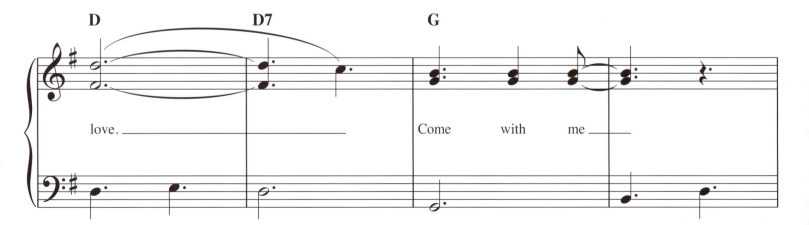

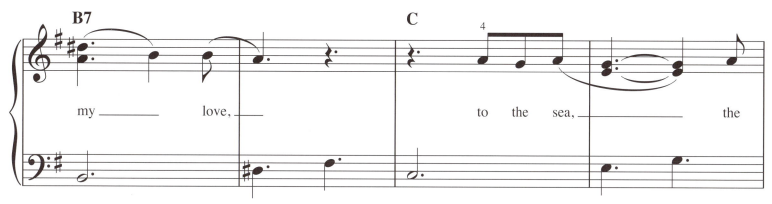

my _____ love, _____ to the sea, _____ the

sea _____ of love. _____ I _____ want to tell you
I _____ want to tell you

just how _____ much I love you. _____
oh, how _____ much I love you. _____

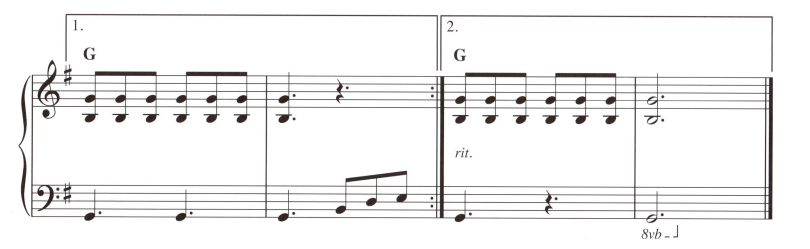

1.

2.

rit.

8vb

SEE YOU LATER, ALLIGATOR

Words and Music by
ROBERT GUIDRY

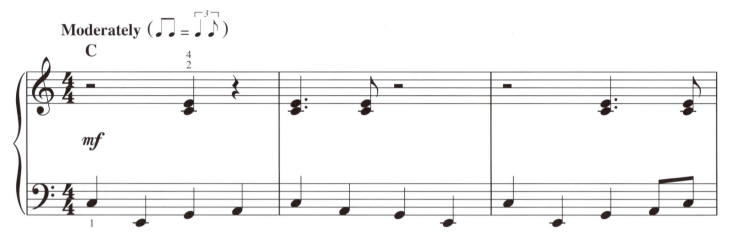

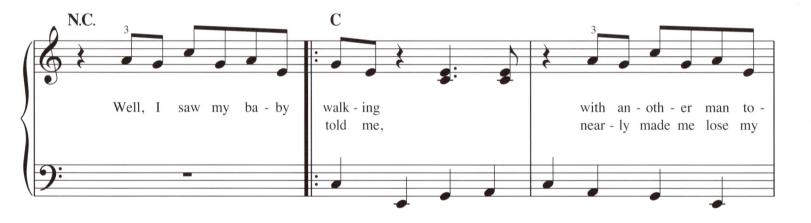

Well, I saw my ba - by walk - ing
told me,

with an - oth - er man to -
near - ly made me lose my

day. ___
head. ___

Well, I saw my ba - by walk - ing
When I thought of what she told me,

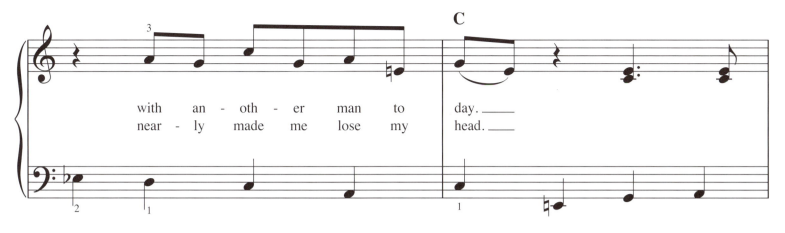

with an - oth - er man to day. ____
near - ly made me lose my head. ____

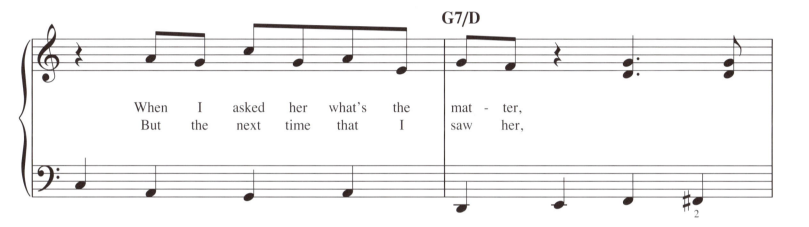

G7/D

When I asked her what's the mat - ter,
But the next time that I saw her,

C   **N.C.**

this is what I heard her say: }
re - mind - ed her of what she said: }

"See you lat - er, al - li -

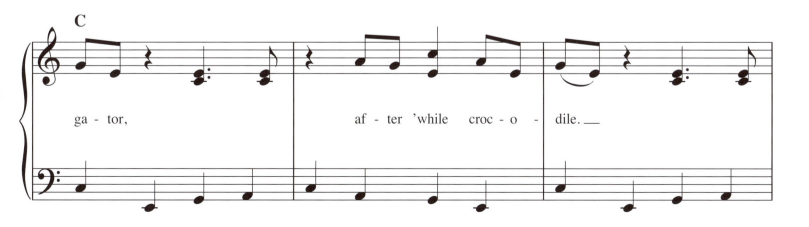

C

ga - tor,   af - ter 'while croc - o - dile. ___

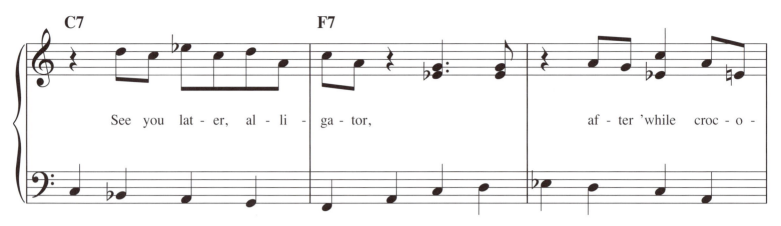

See you lat - er, al - li - ga - tor, af - ter 'while croc - o -

dile. ___ Can't you see you're in my way, now,

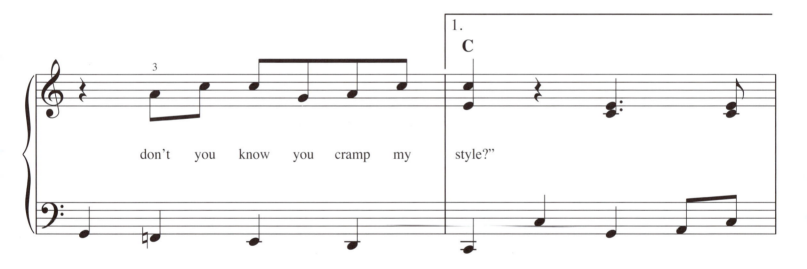

don't you know you cramp my style?"

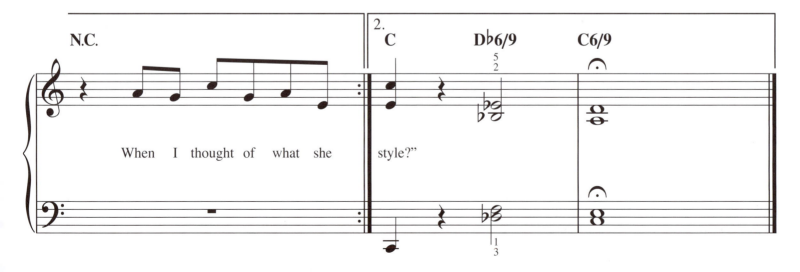

When I thought of what she style?"

SPLISH SPLASH

Words and Music by BOBBY DARIN
and MURRAY KAUFMAN

Moderately, with a beat

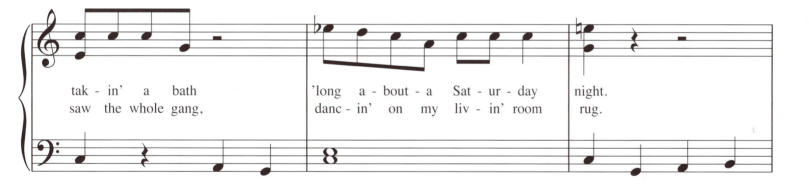

Splish splash, I was
Bing bang, ___ I

tak - in' a bath   'long a - bout a Sat - ur - day   night.
saw the whole gang,   danc - in' on my liv - in' room   rug.

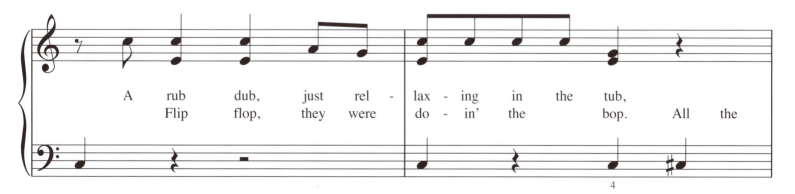

A rub dub, just rel - lax - ing in the tub,
Flip flop, they were do - in' the bop. All the

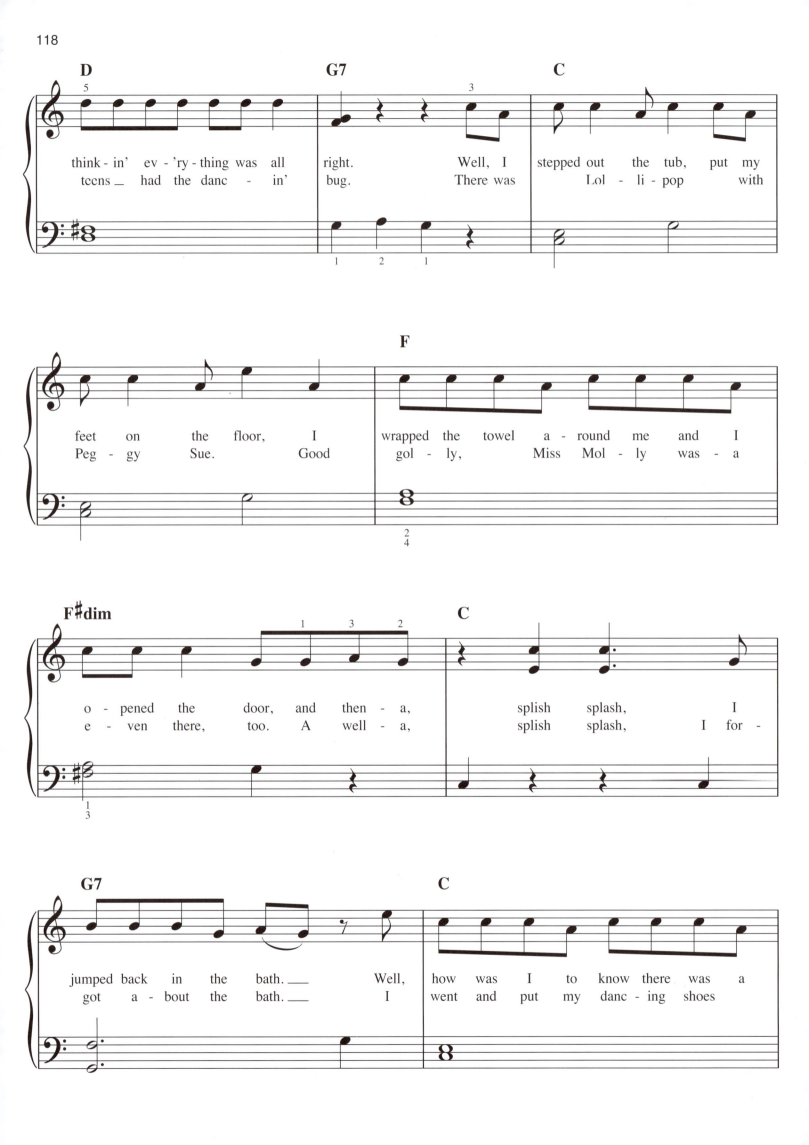

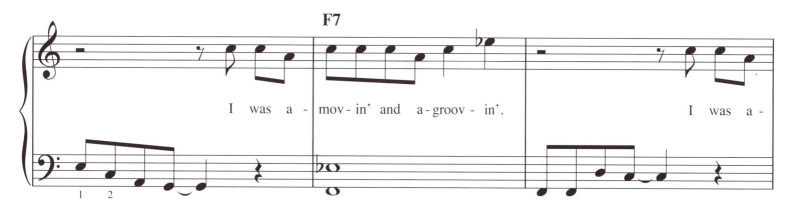

SH-BOOM

Words and Music by JAMES KEYES,
CLAUDE FEASTER, CARL FEASTER,
FLOYD McRAE and JAMES EDWARDS

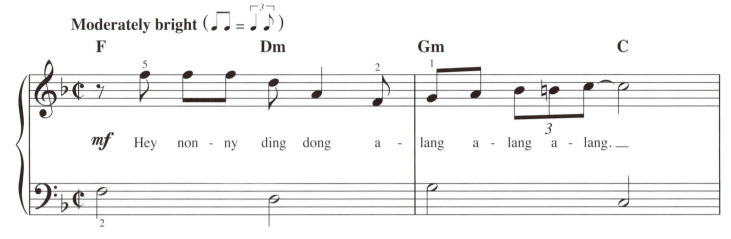

Hey non - ny ding dong a - lang a - lang a - lang.

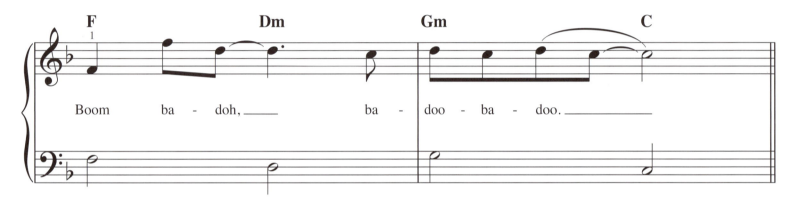

Boom ba - doh, _____ ba - doo - ba - doo. _____

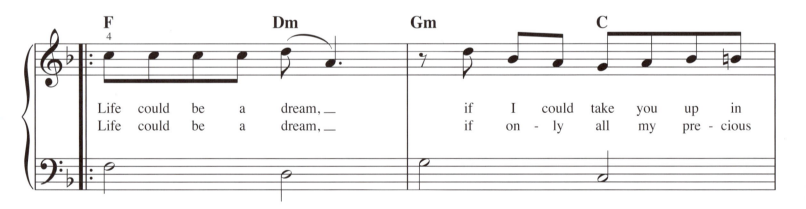

Life could be a dream, ___ if I could take you up in
Life could be a dream, ___ if on - ly all my pre - cious

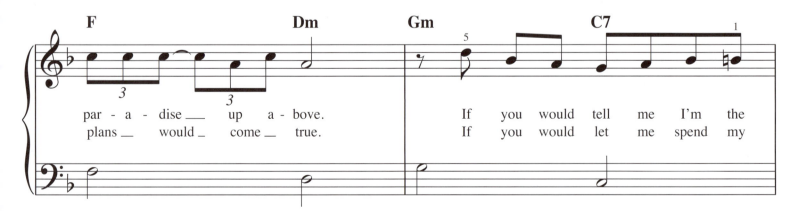

par - a - dise ___ up a - bove.   If you would tell me I'm the
plans ___ would ___ come ___ true.   If you would let me spend my

on - ly one that you love,   life could be a dream, __ sweet -
whole life ___ lov - in' you,   life could be a dream, __ sweet -

1.

heart. Hel - lo, hel - lo a - gain, __ sh - boom, and hop - in' we'll meet a - gain.

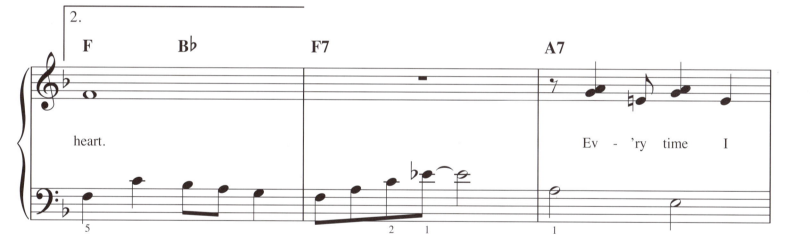

2.

heart.   Ev - 'ry time I

look at you ___   some - thing is on my mind. __

If you'd do what I want you to, _____

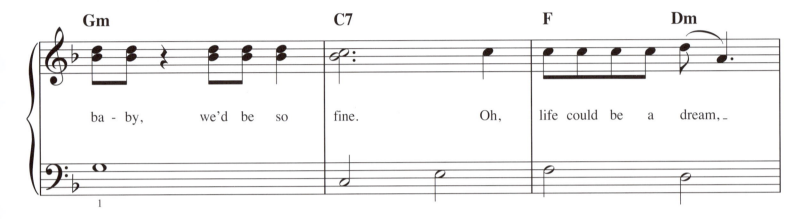

ba - by, we'd be so fine. Oh, life could be a dream, __

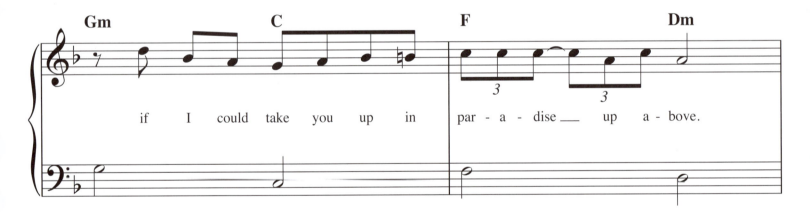

if I could take you up in par - a - dise __ up a - bove.

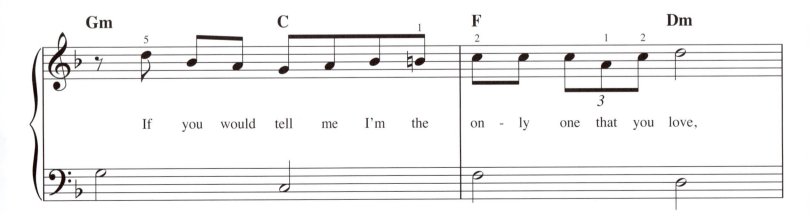

If you would tell me I'm the on - ly one that you love,

life could be a dream, __ sweet - heart. Sh - boom, __

ya da da da da da da da da da. Sh - boom sh - boom, __

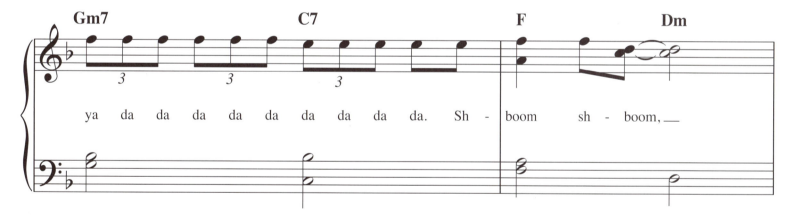

ya da da da da da da da da da. Sh - boom sh - boom, __

life could be a dream, __ sweet - heart.

SILHOUETTES

Words and Music by FRANK C. SLAY JR.
and BOB CREWE

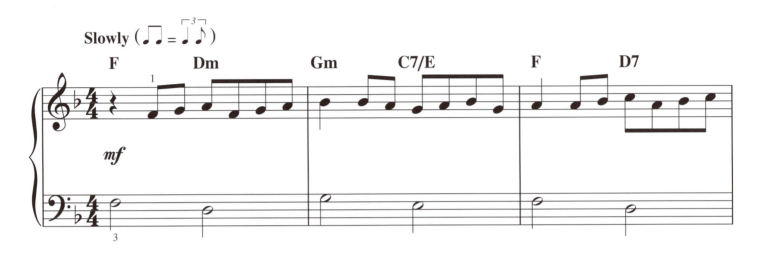

Took a walk and passed your house late last

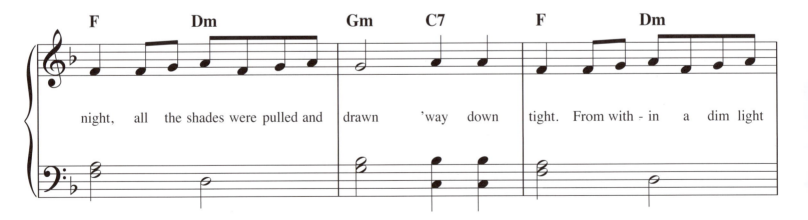

night, all the shades were pulled and drawn 'way down tight. From with-in a dim light

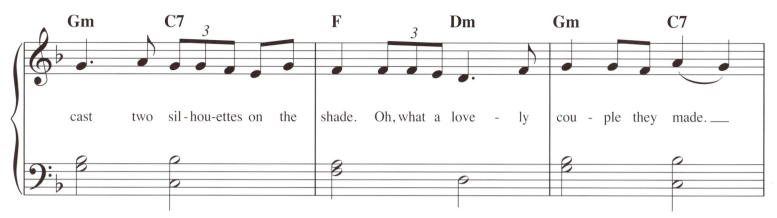

cast two sil-hou-ettes on the shade. Oh, what a love - ly cou - ple they made. ___

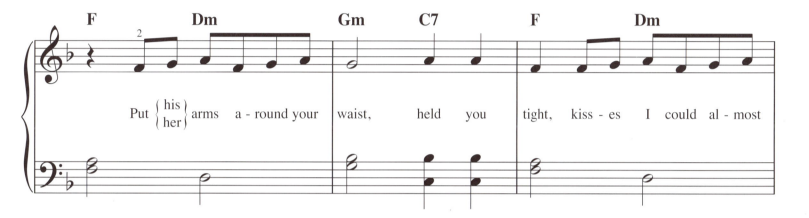

Put {his}/{her} arms a - round your waist, held you tight, kiss - es I could al - most

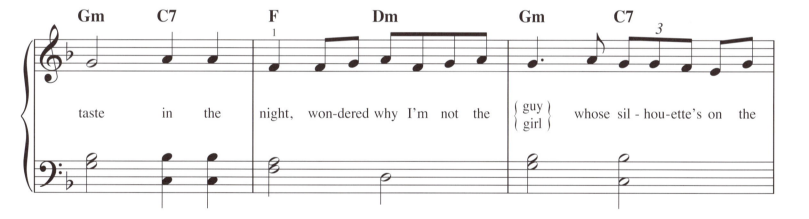

taste in the night, won-dered why I'm not the {guy}/{girl} whose sil - hou-ette's on the

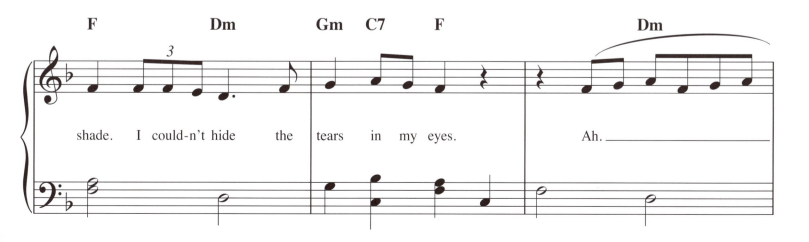

shade. I could-n't hide the tears in my eyes. Ah. ___

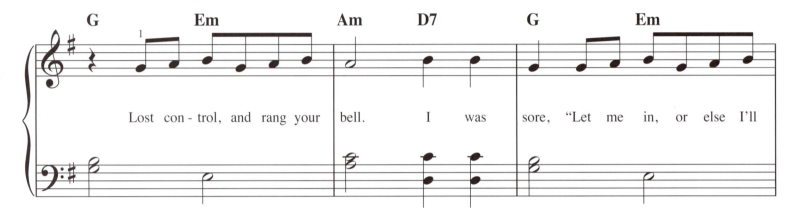

Lost con - trol, and rang your bell. I was sore, "Let me in, or else I'll

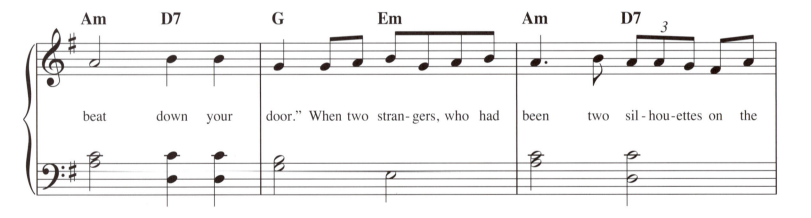

beat down your door." When two stran - gers, who had been two sil - hou - ettes on the

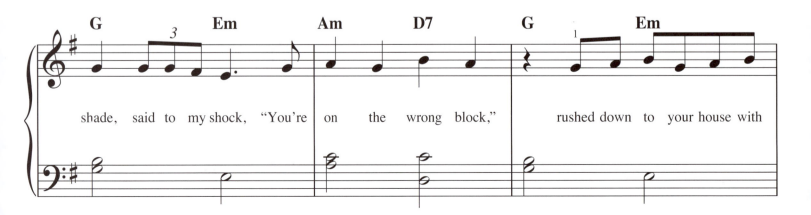

shade, said to my shock, "You're on the wrong block," rushed down to your house with

wings   on   my   feet. Loved you like I've nev - er   loved   you   my

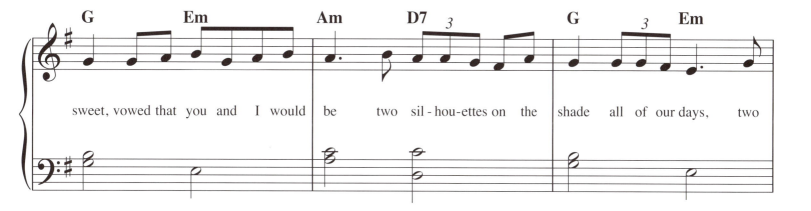

sweet, vowed that you and I would   be   two sil-hou-ettes on the   shade   all of our days,   two

sil - hou-ettes on the shade.   Ah._____

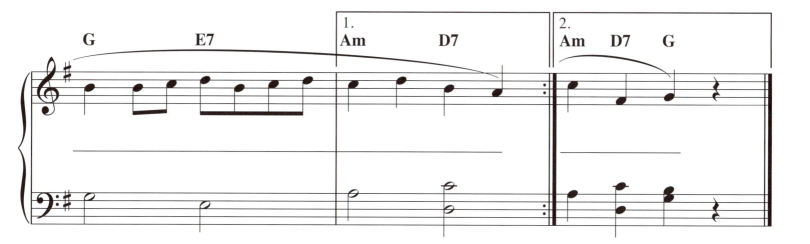

THE STROLL

Words and Music by CLYDE OTIS
and NANCY LEE

Slowly, with a strong beat

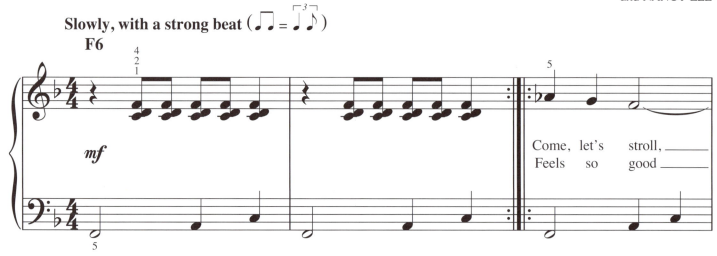

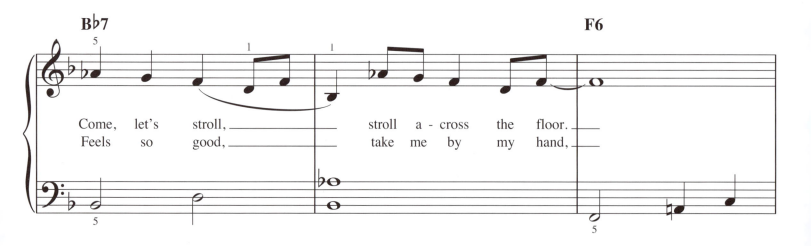

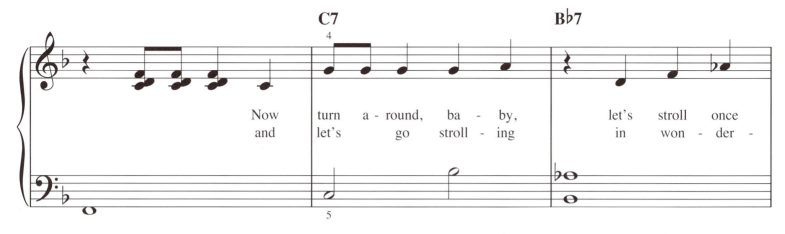

Now turn a-round, ba - by, let's stroll once
and let's go stroll - ing in won - der -

more. Stroll - ing,
land.

stroll - ing, rock and roll - ing,

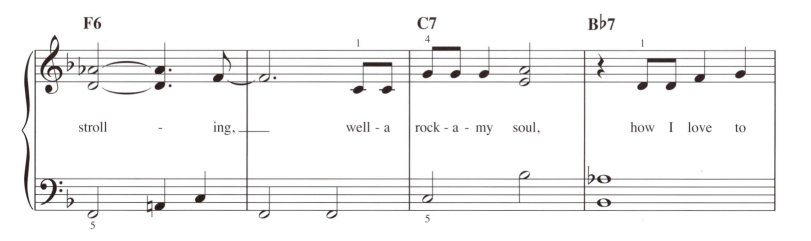

stroll - ing, well - a rock-a-my soul, how I love to

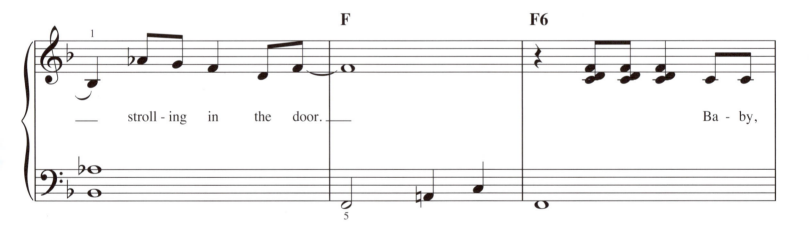

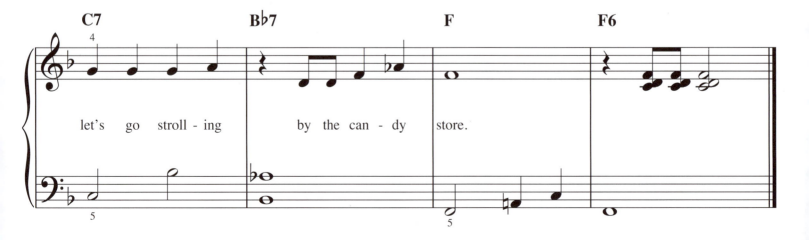

UNDER THE BOARDWALK

Words and Music by ARTIE RESNICK
and KENNY YOUNG

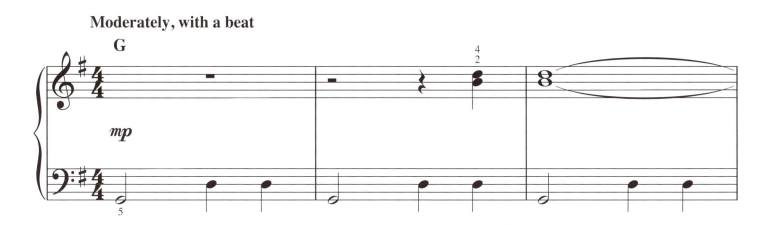

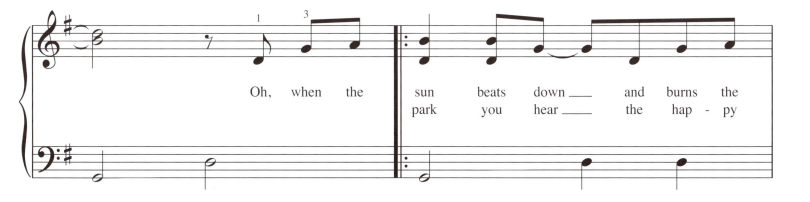

Oh, when the sun beats down ___ and burns the
park you hear ___ the hap-py

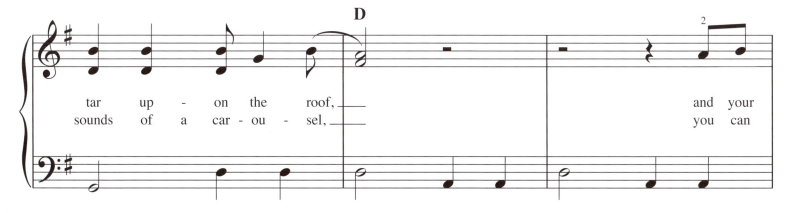

tar up - on the roof, ___
sounds of a car - ou - sel, ___
and your
you can

shoes get so hot you wish your tired feet were fire -
al - most taste the hot dogs and french fries they

proof. Un - der the board - walk, __
sell.

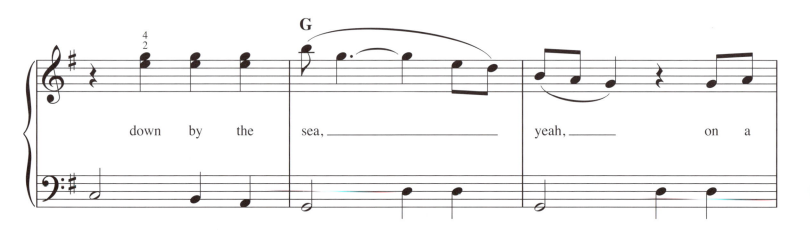

down by the sea, _____ yeah, _____ on a

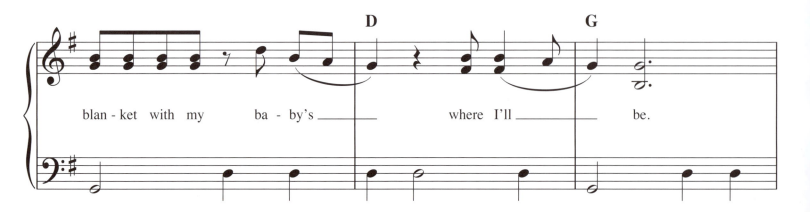

blan - ket with my ba - by's ____ where I'll ____ be.

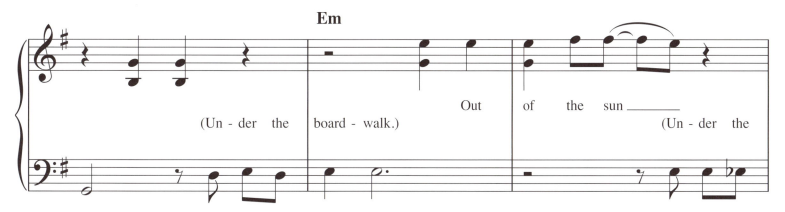

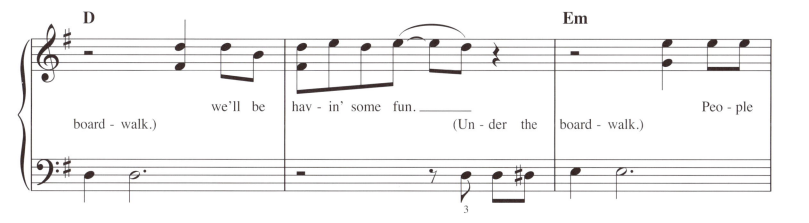

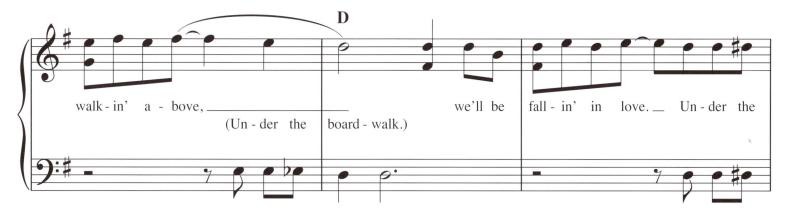

A TEENAGER IN LOVE

Words by DOC POMUS
Music by MORT SHUMAN

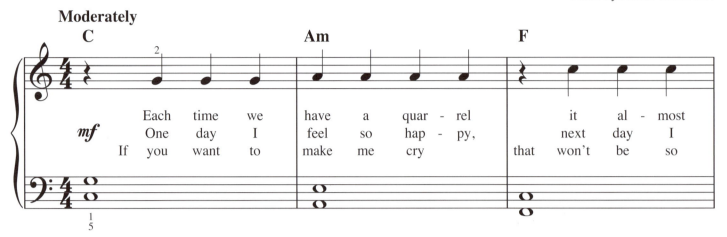

Moderately

Each time we have a quar - rel it al - most
One day I make me cry that next day I
If you want to feel so hap - py, that won't be so

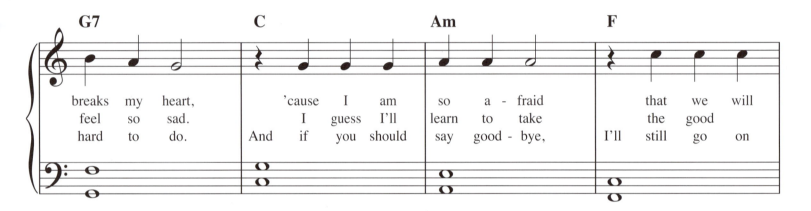

breaks my heart, 'cause I am so a - fraid that we will
feel so sad. I guess I'll learn to take the good
hard to do. And if you should say good - bye, I'll still go on

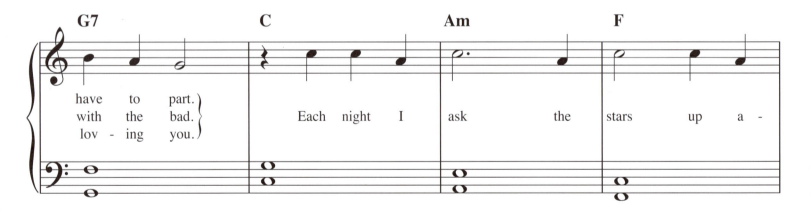

have to part. Each night I ask the stars up a -
with the bad.
lov - ing you.

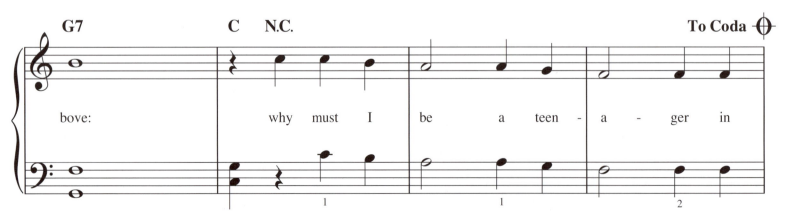

To Coda

bove: why must I be a teen - a - ger in

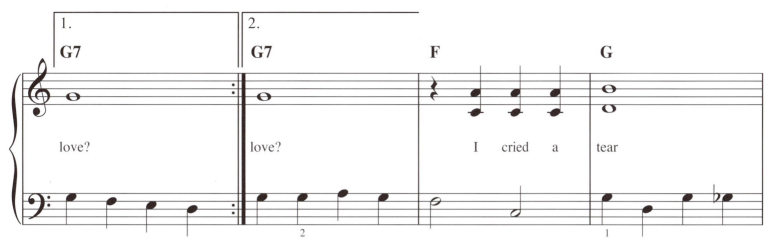

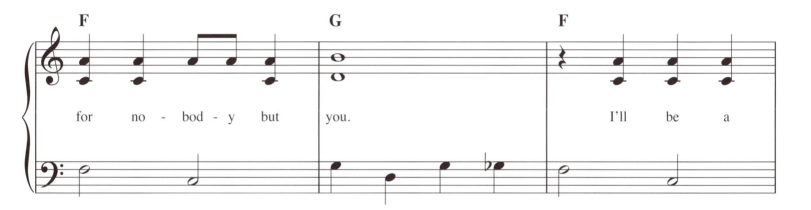

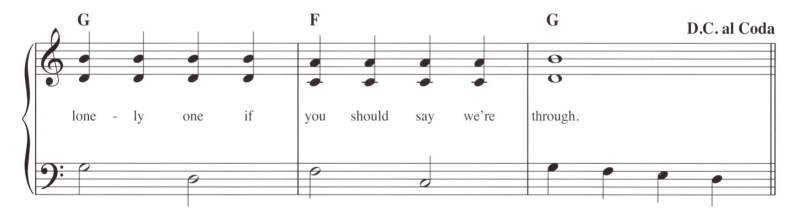

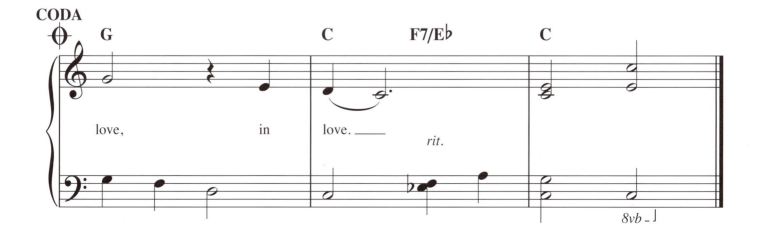

TEQUILA

By CHUCK RIO

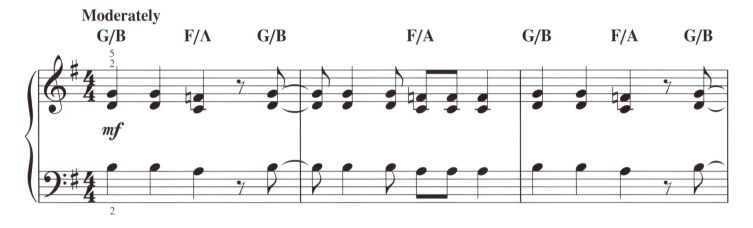

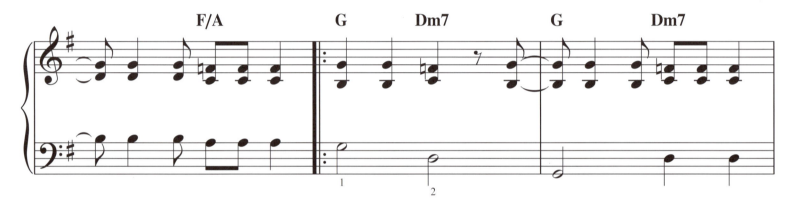

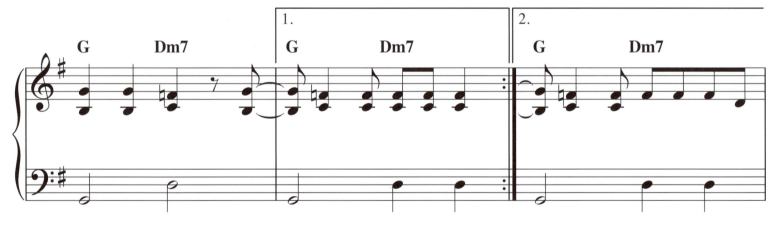

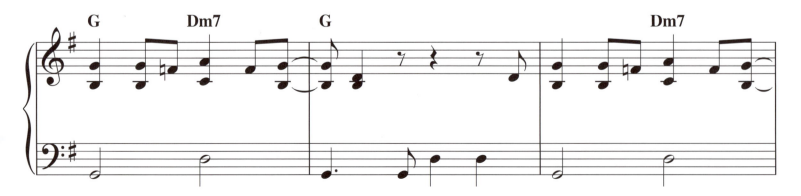

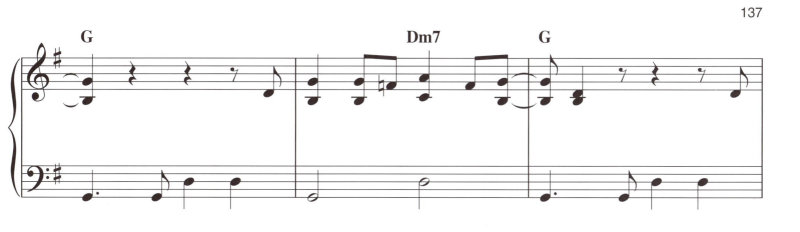

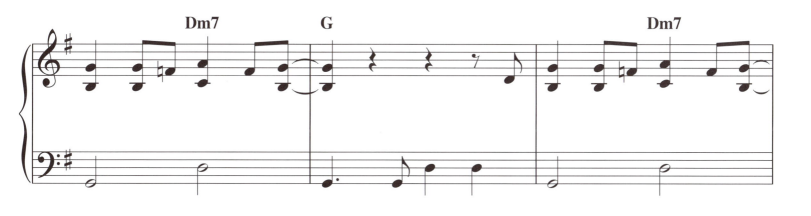

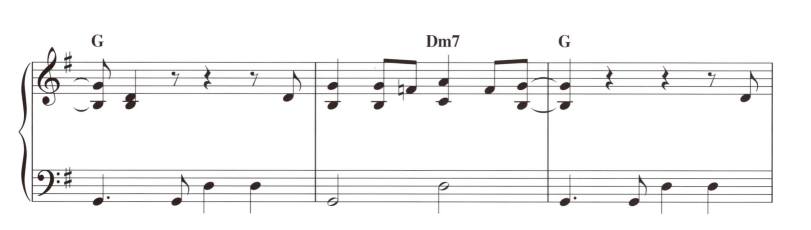

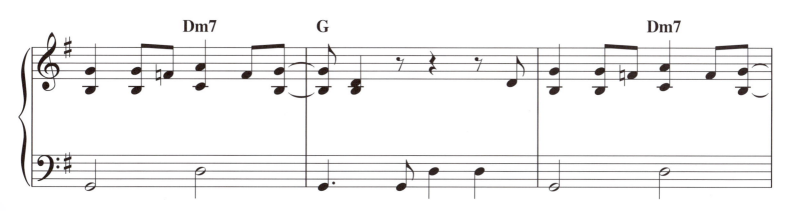

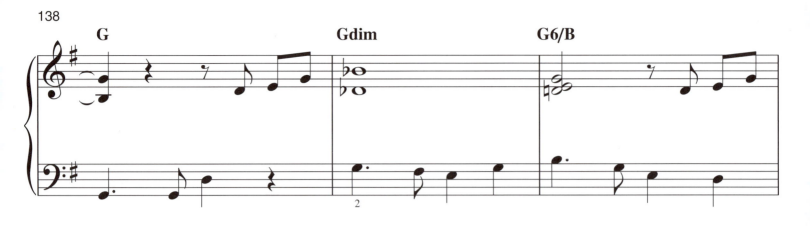

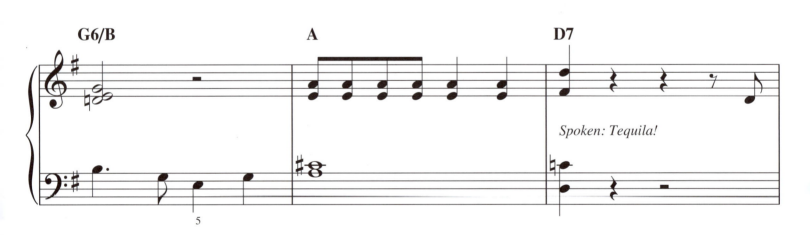

Spoken: Tequila!

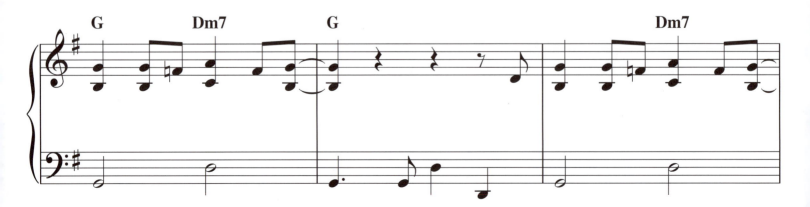

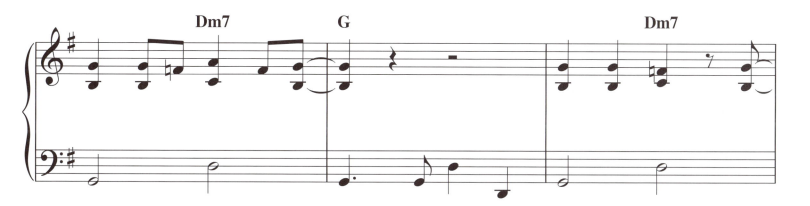

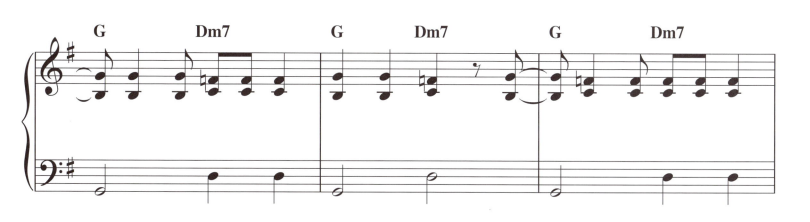

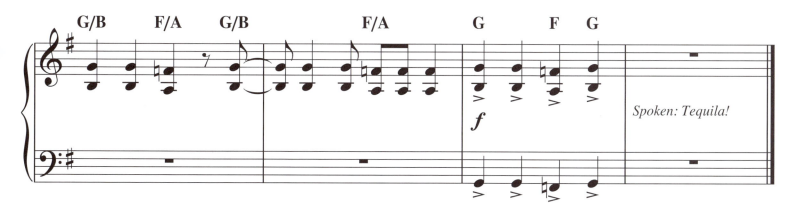

Spoken: Tequila!

TONIGHT YOU BELONG TO ME

Words by BILLY ROSE
Music by LEE DAVID

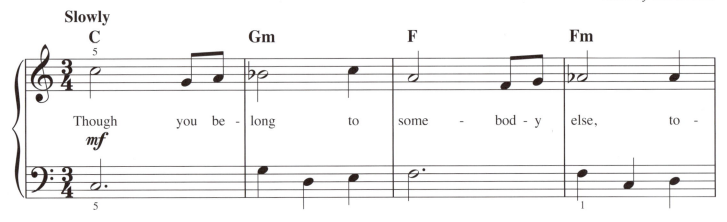

Though you be - long to some - bod - y else, to -

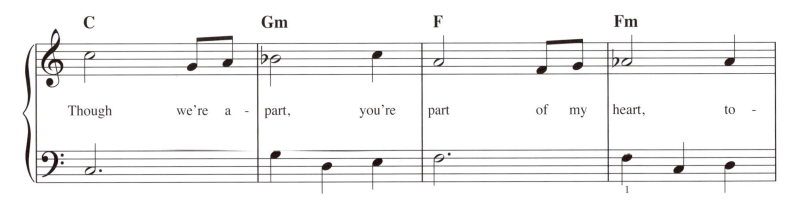

night you be - long to me.

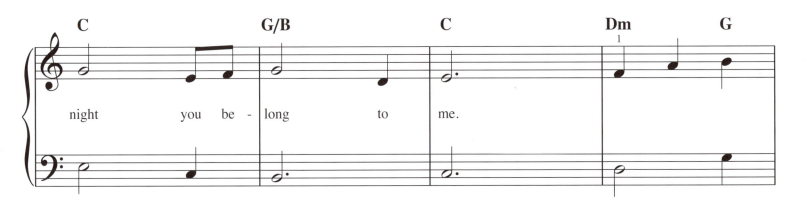

Though we're a - part, you're part of my heart, to -

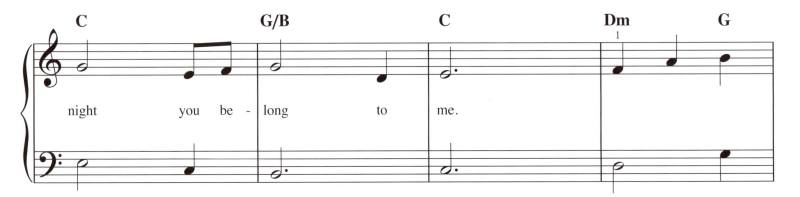

night you be - long to me.

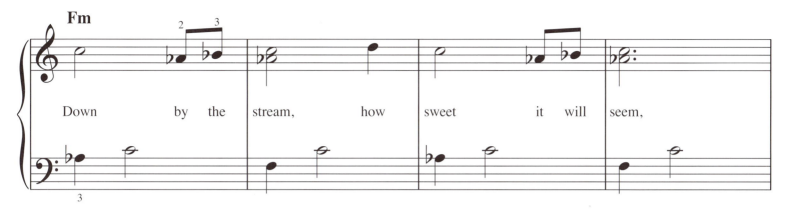

Down   by the   stream,   how   sweet   it will   seem,

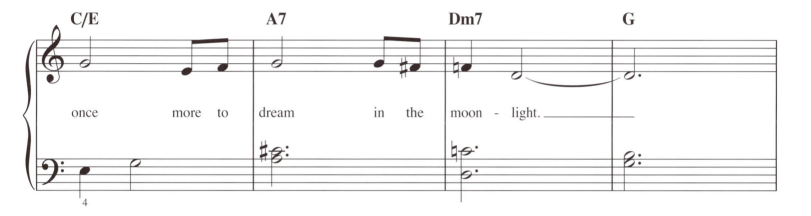

once   more to   dream   in the   moon - light.

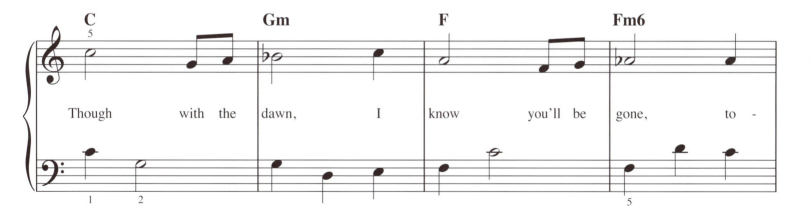

Though   with the   dawn,   I   know   you'll be   gone,   to -

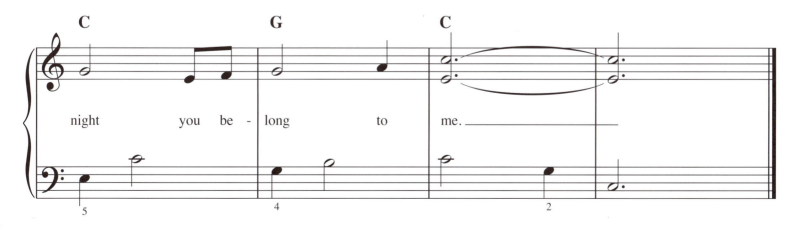

night   you be - long   to   me.

TOO MUCH

Words and Music by LEE ROSENBERG
and BERNARD WEINMAN

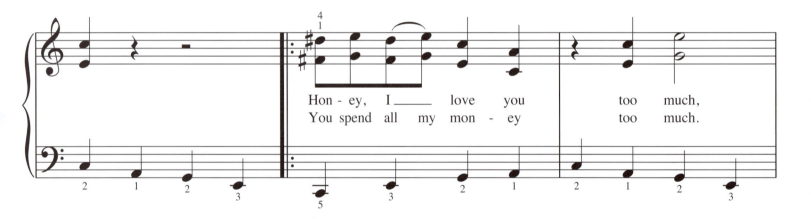

Hon - ey, I ___ love you   too   much,
You spend all my mon - ey   too   much.

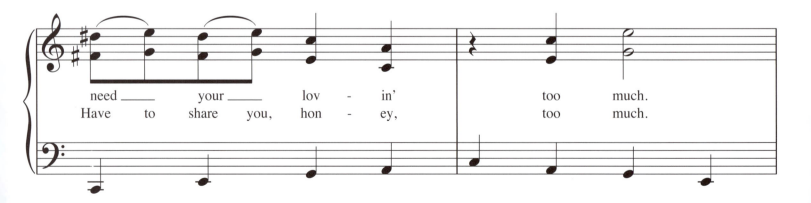

need ___ your ___ lov - in'   too   much.
Have to share you, hon - ey,   too   much.

Want ____ the ____ thrill of your touch.
When I want some lov - in', you're gone.

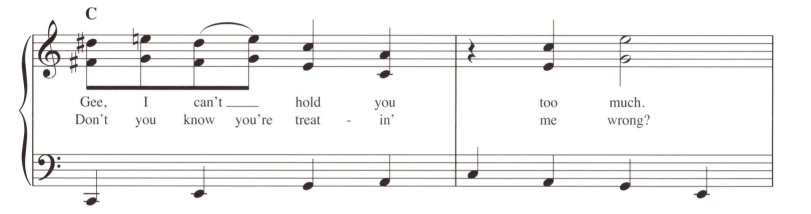

Gee, I can't ____ hold you too much.
Don't you know you're treat - in' me wrong?

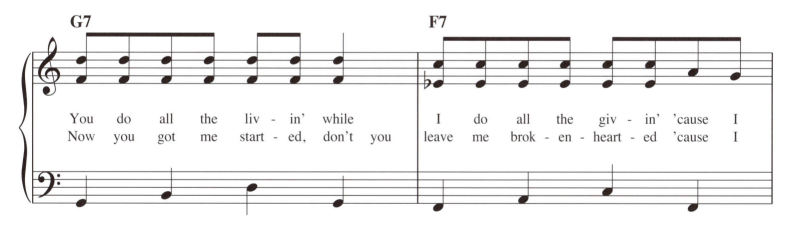

You do all the liv - in' while I do all the giv - in' 'cause I
Now you got me start - ed, don't you leave me brok - en - heart - ed 'cause I

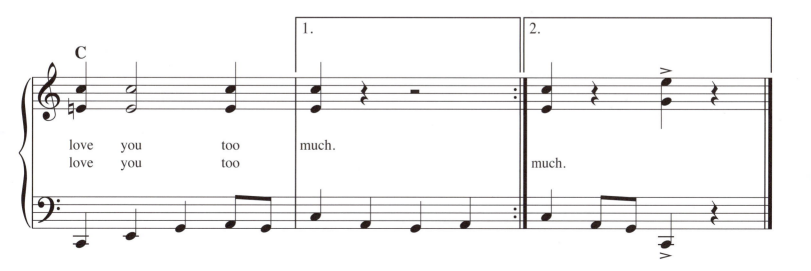

love you too much.
love you too much.

TUTTI FRUTTI

Words and Music by LITTLE RICHARD PENNIMAN
and DOROTHY LA BOSTRIE

Bright Rock

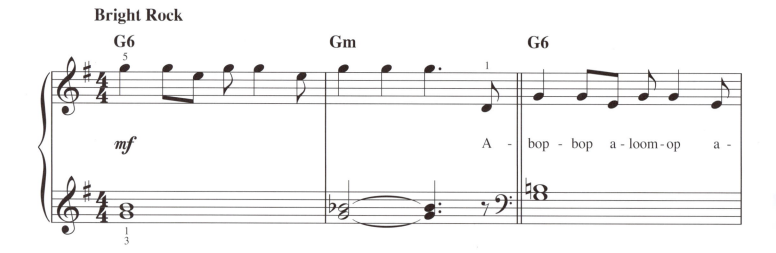

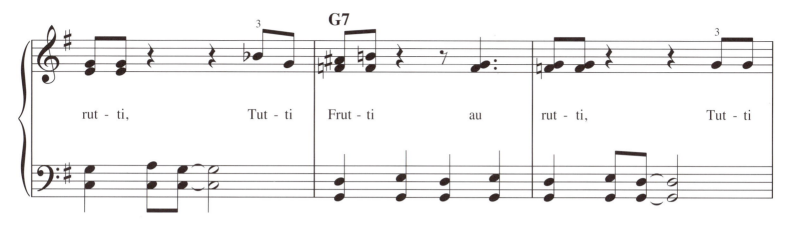

rut - ti,   Tut - ti   Frut - ti   au   rut - ti,   Tut - ti

Frut - ti   au   rut - ti,   A - bop - bop a - loom - op a -

lop   bop   boom! I got a   gal,   her name's
                        gal,   her name's

Sue,   she knows just what to do.   I got a
Dai - sy,   she al - most drives me cra - zy.   I got a

146

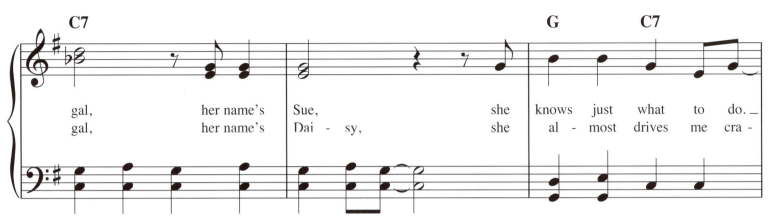

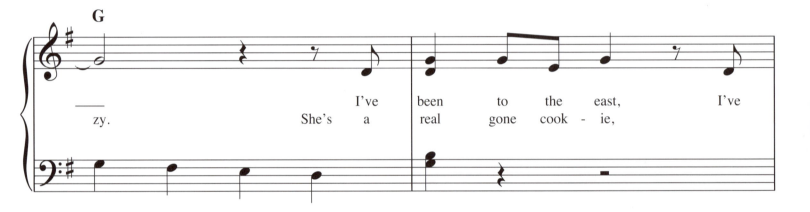

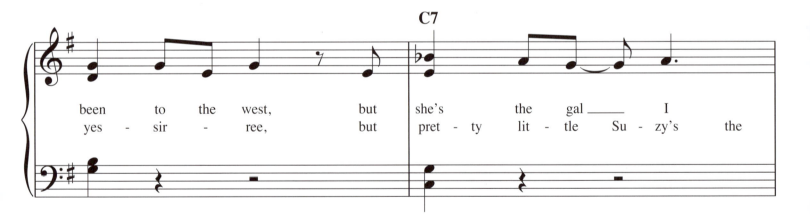

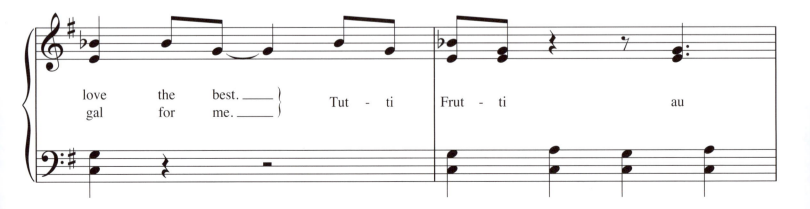

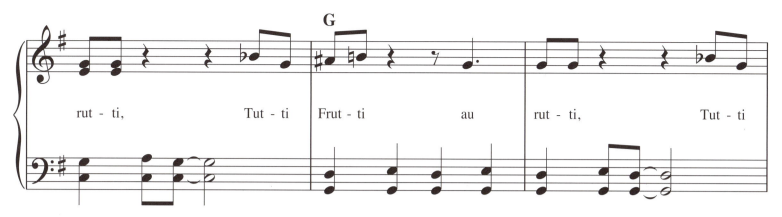

rut - ti,   Tut - ti Frut - ti au   rut - ti,   Tut - ti

Frut - ti   au   rut - ti,   Tut - ti Frut - ti   au

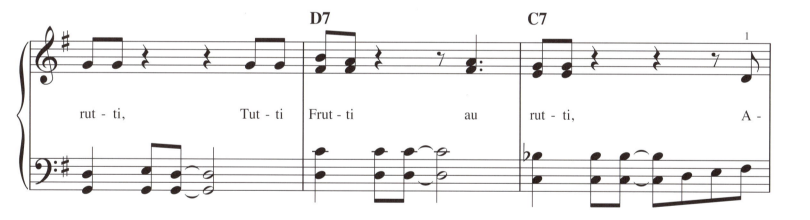

rut - ti,   Tut - ti Frut - ti   au   rut - ti,   A -

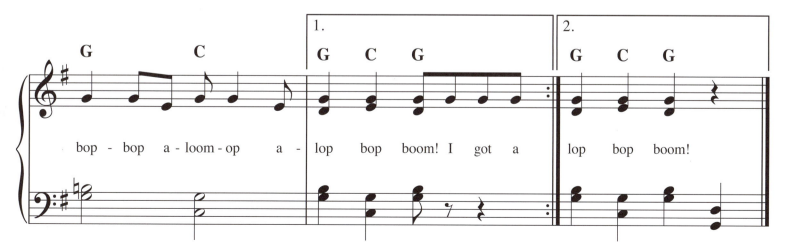

bop - bop a - loom - op a - lop bop boom! I got a   lop bop boom!

TWEEDLE DEE

Words and Music by
WINFIELD SCOTT

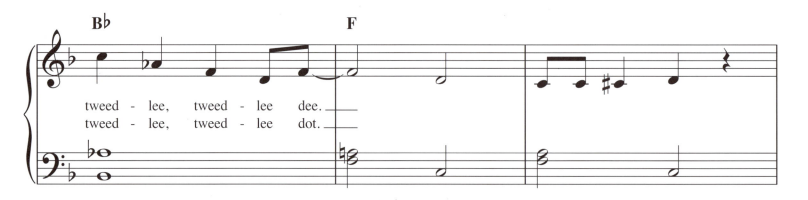

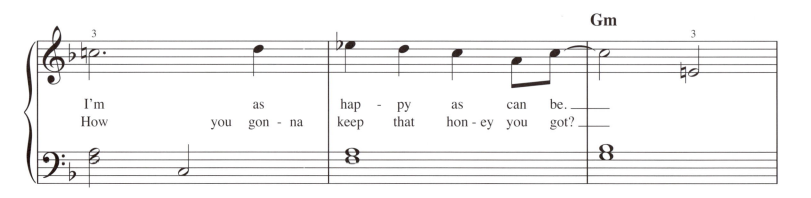

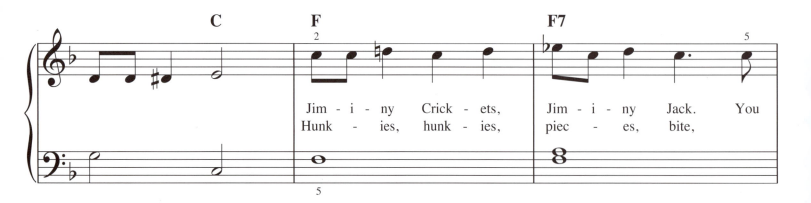

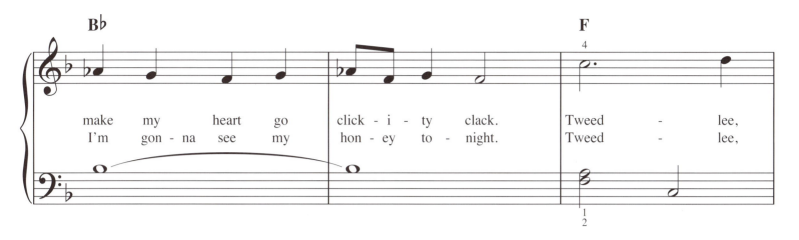

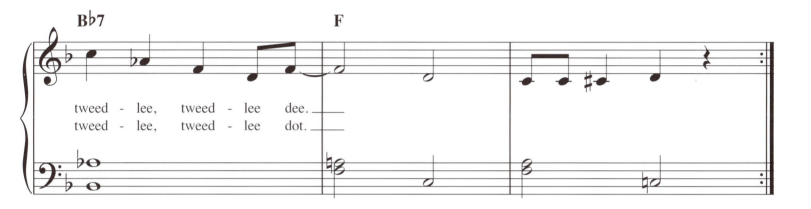

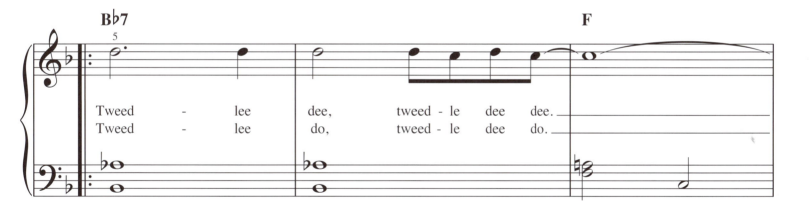

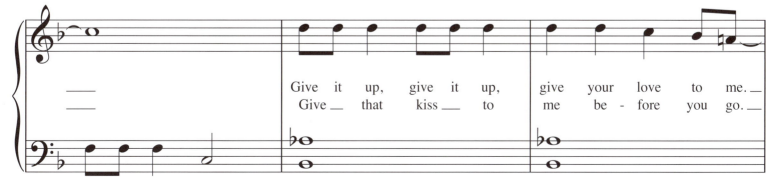

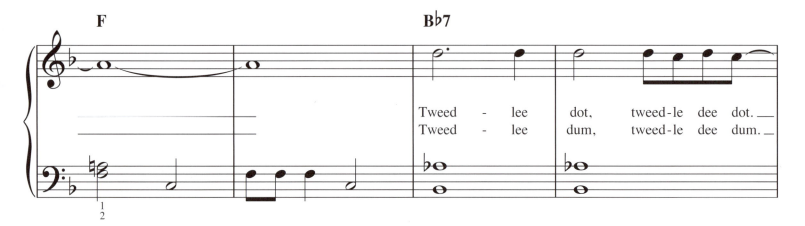

Tweed - lee dot, tweed-le dee dot.__
Tweed - lee dum, tweed-le dee dum.__

Gim - me, gim - me, gim - me, gim - me,
Look - ie, look - ie, look - ie, look - ie,

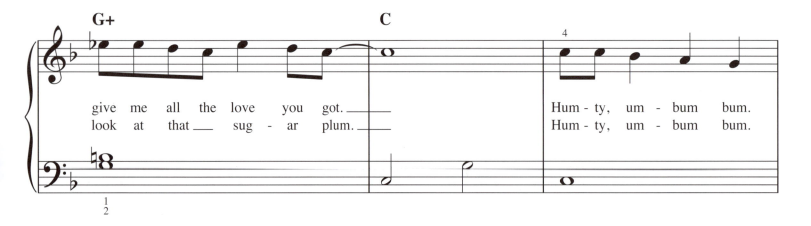

give me all the love you got.__
look at that__ sug - ar plum.__

Hum - ty, um - bum bum.
Hum - ty, um - bum bum.

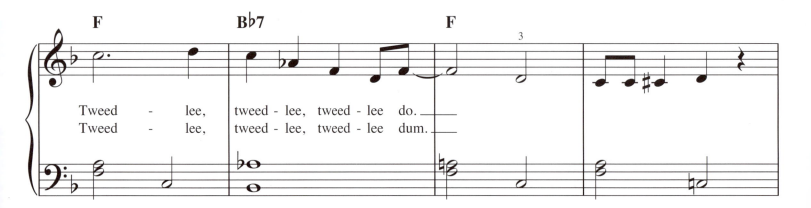

Tweed - lee, tweed - lee, tweed - lee do.__
Tweed - lee, tweed - lee, tweed - lee dum.__

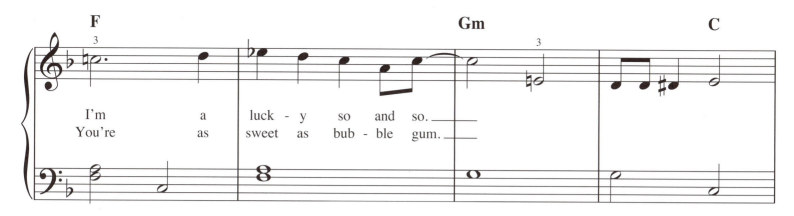

I'm   a   luck - y   so   and   so. _____
You're   as   sweet   as   bub - ble   gum. _____

Hub - ba,   hub - ba,   hon - ey,   do, _____   I'm   gon - na   keep   my
Mer - cy,   mer - cy   pud - din'   pie, _____   you've   got _____ some - thin' that

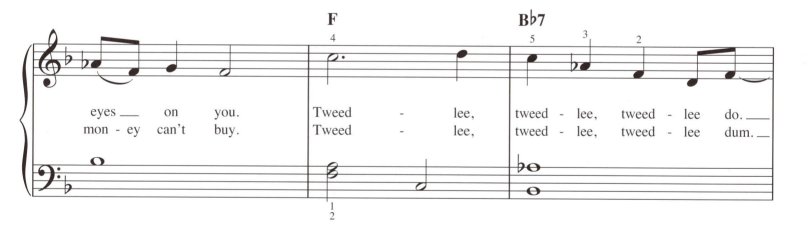

eyes _____ on   you.   Tweed - lee,   tweed - lee,   tweed - lee   do. _____
mon - ey   can't   buy.   Tweed - lee,   tweed - lee,   tweed - lee   dum. _____

26 MILES
(Santa Catalina)

Words and Music by GLEN LARSON
and BRUCE BELLAND

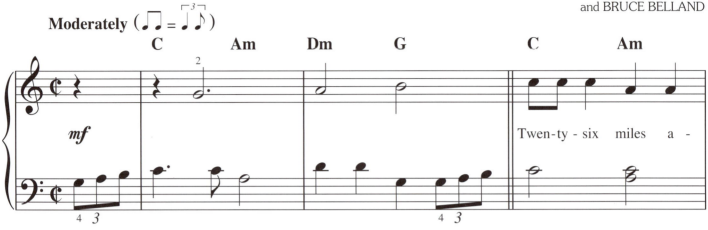

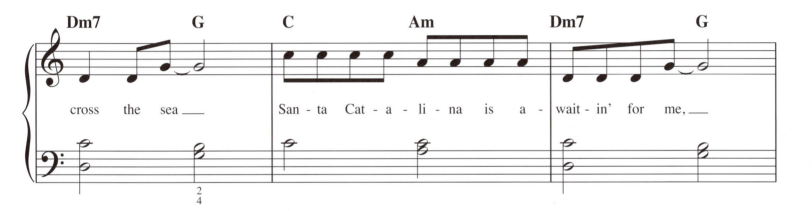

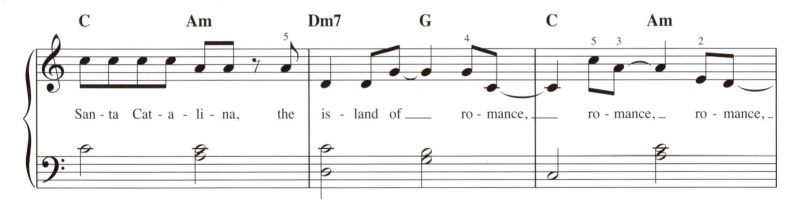

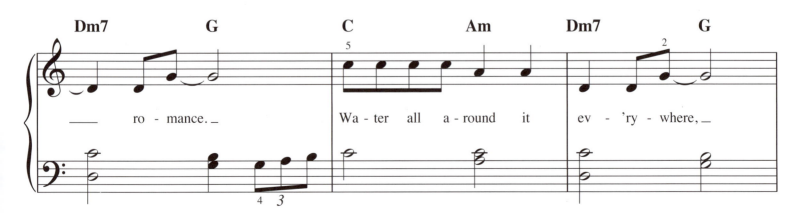

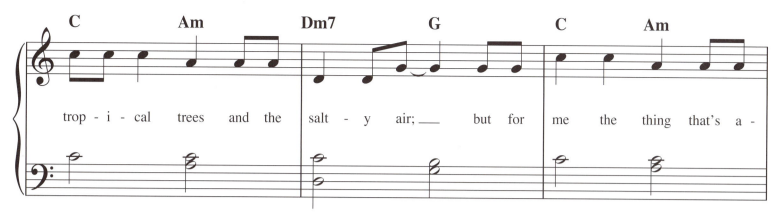

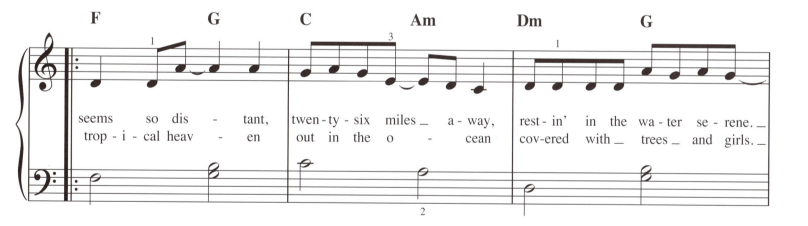

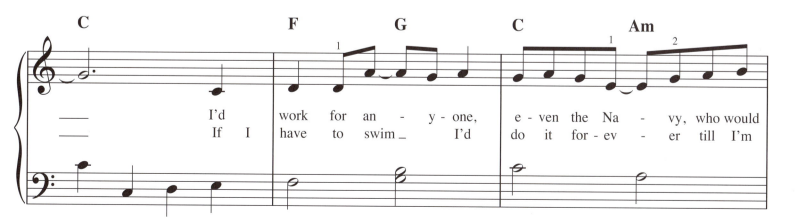

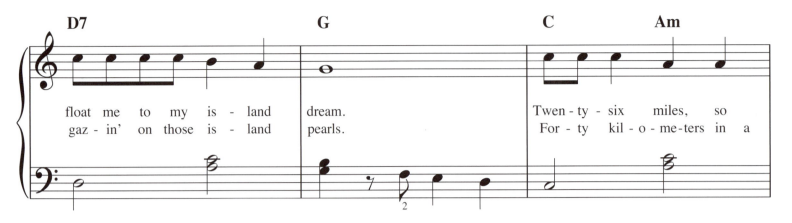

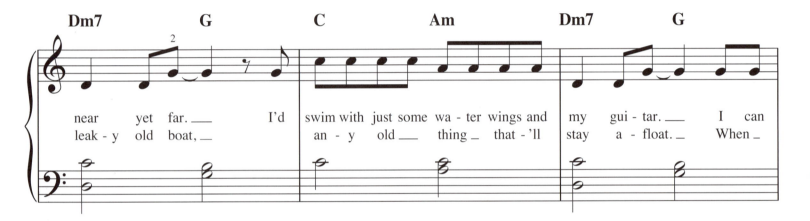

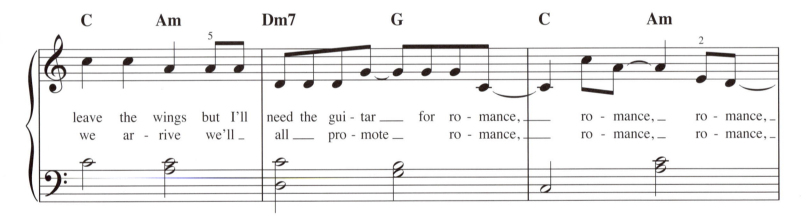

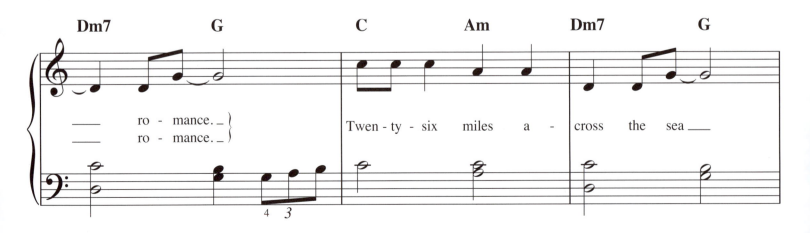

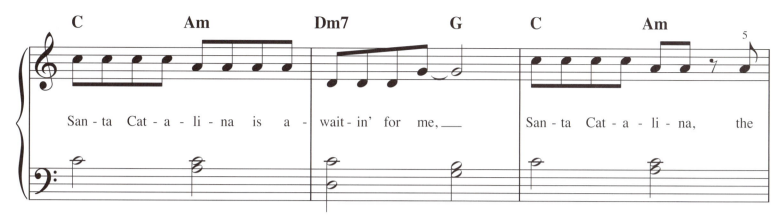

Santa Cat - a - li - na is a - wait - in' for me, ___ San - ta Cat - a - li - na, the

is - land of ___ ro - mance, ___

A

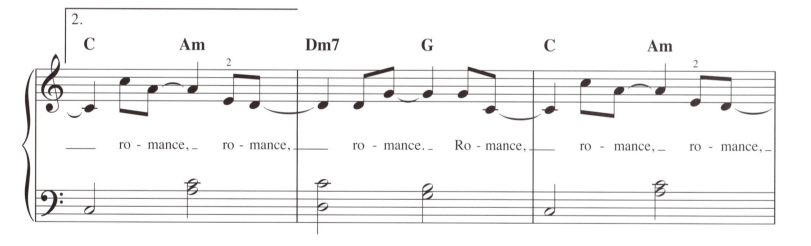

___ ro - mance, _ ro - mance, ___ ro - mance. _ Ro - mance, _ ro - mance, _ ro - mance, _

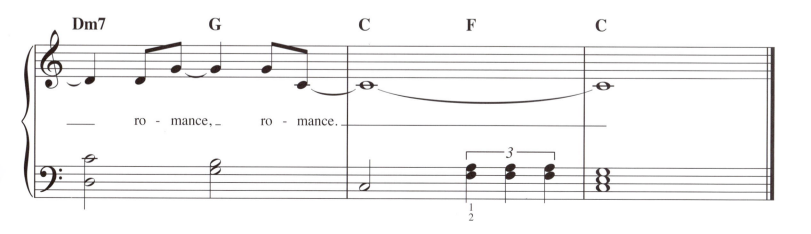

___ ro - mance, _ ro - mance.

TWIST AND SHOUT

Words and Music by BERT RUSSELL
and PHIL MEDLEY

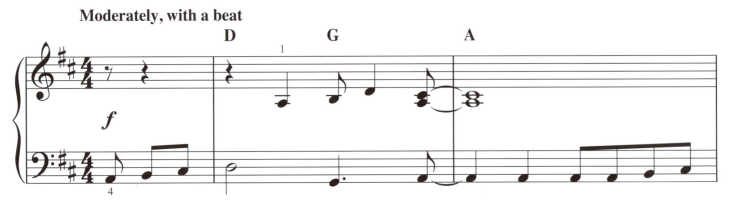

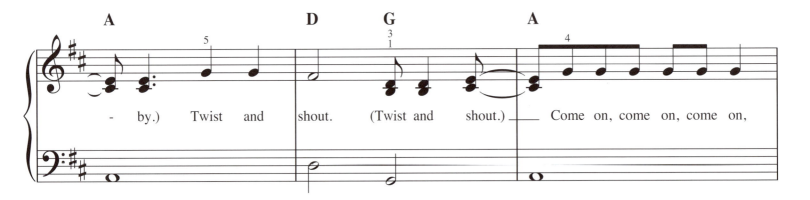

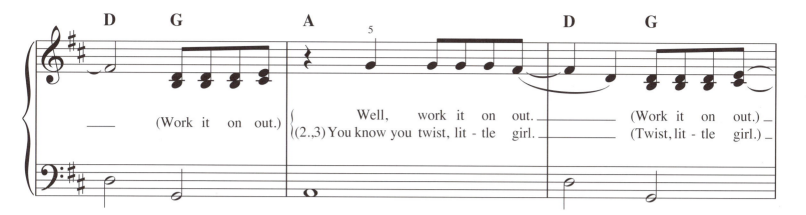

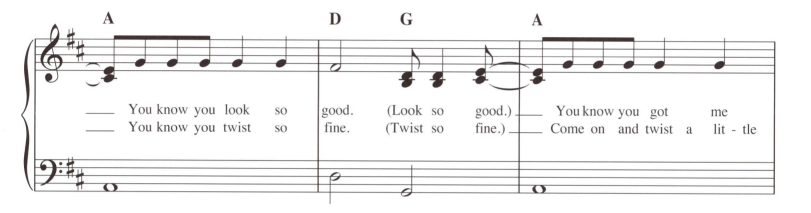

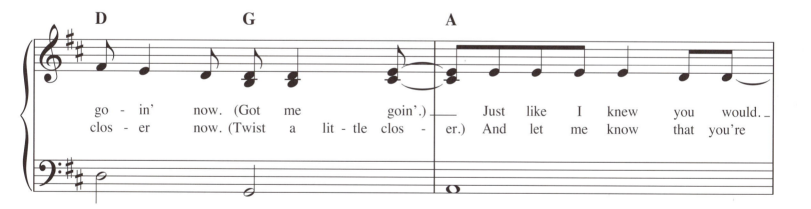

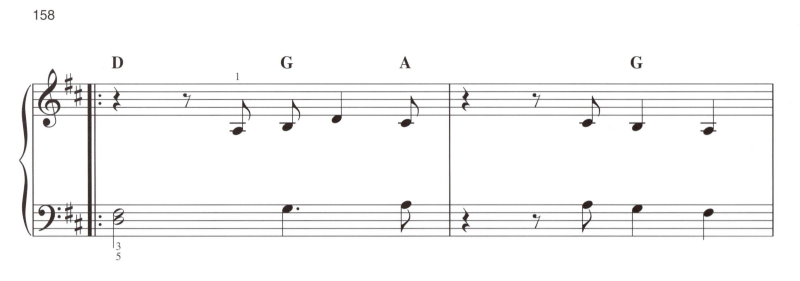

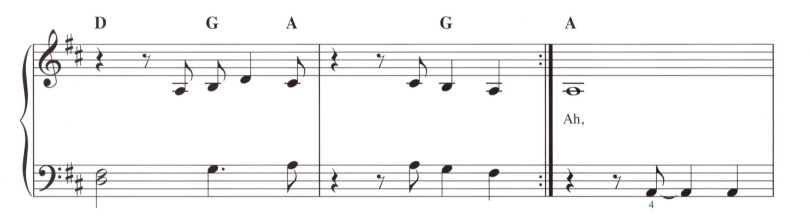

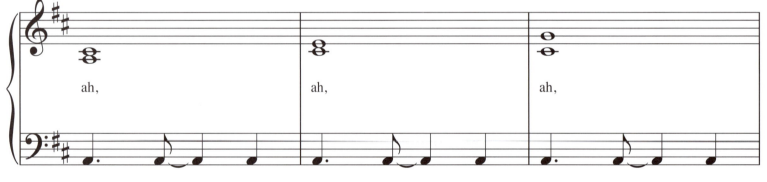

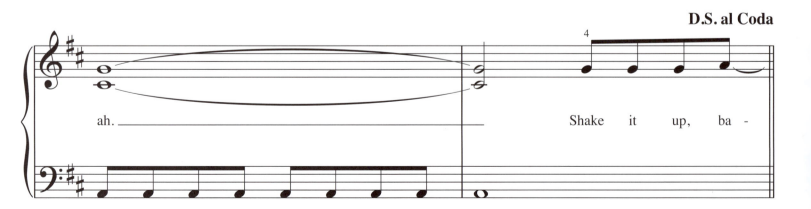

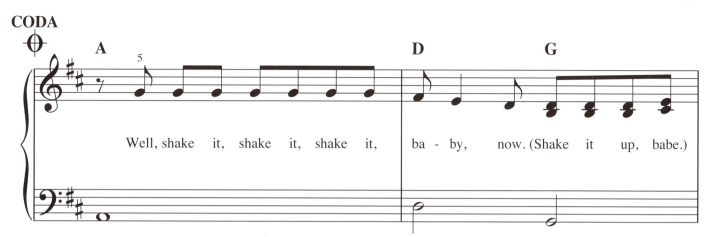

Well, shake it, shake it, shake it, ba - by, now. (Shake it up, babe.)

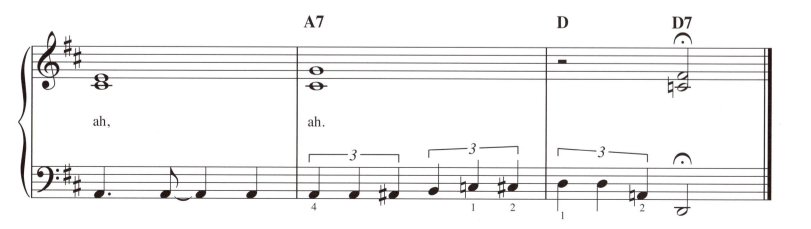

Well, shake it, shake it, shake it ba - by, now. (Shake it up, babe.)

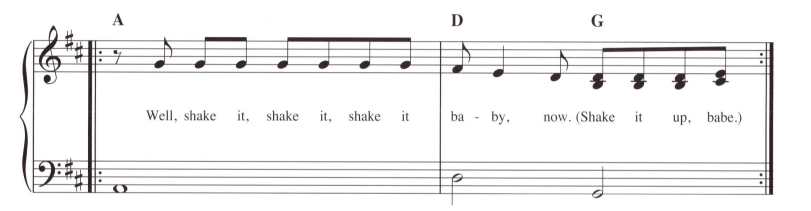

Oo.   Ah,   ah,

ah,   ah.

THE WANDERER

Words and Music by
ERNEST MARESCA

Oh well,

I'm the type of guy ____ that would | nev - er set - tle down. ____ | Where
Flo on my left arm, ____ and there's | Mar - y on my right, ____ | and
I'm the type of guy ____ that ____ | likes to roam a - round. ____ | I'm

pret - ty girls are, ____ well, you | know that I'm a - round. ____ | I
Ja - nie is the girl, ____ well, that | I'll be with to - night. ____ | And
nev - er in one place, ____ I ____ | go from town to town. ____ | And

F7

kiss them and hug them, 'cause to | me they're all the same. ___ I
when she asks me which one that | I ___ love the best, ___ I'll
when I find my - self ___ | fall - ing for a girl, ___ I

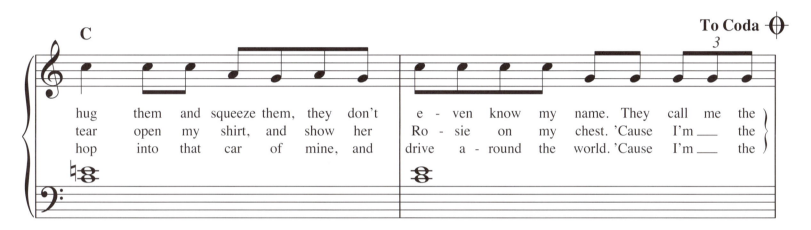

C **To Coda** ⊕

hug them and squeeze them, they don't | e - ven know my name. They call me the
tear open my shirt, and show her | Ro - sie on my chest. 'Cause I'm ___ the
hop into that car of mine, and | drive a - round the world. 'Cause I'm ___ the

G7 **F7**

wan - der - er, ___ oh yeah, the | wan - der - er. ___ I roam a -

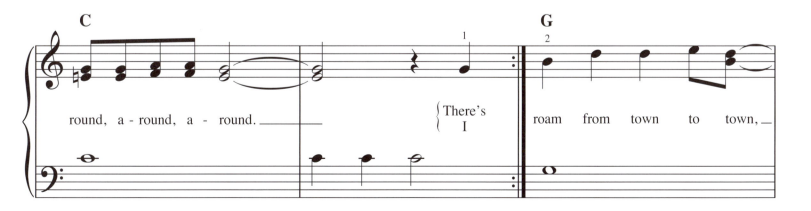

C **G**

round, a - round, a - round. ___ | There's | roam from town to town, ___
| I |

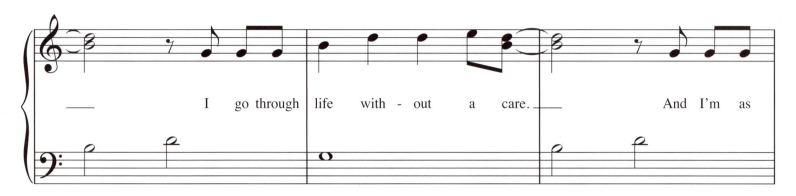

I go through life with-out a care. ___ And I'm as

hap - py as a clown ___ with my two fists of i - ron but I'm

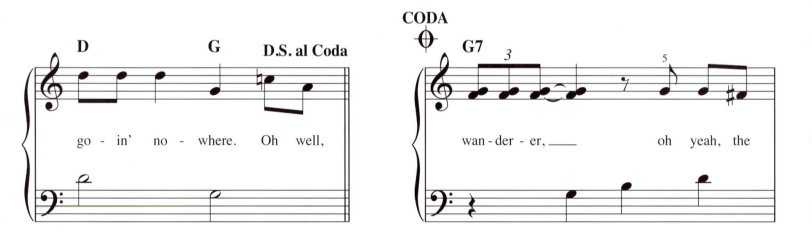

go - in' no - where. Oh well,

wan - der - er, ___ oh yeah, the

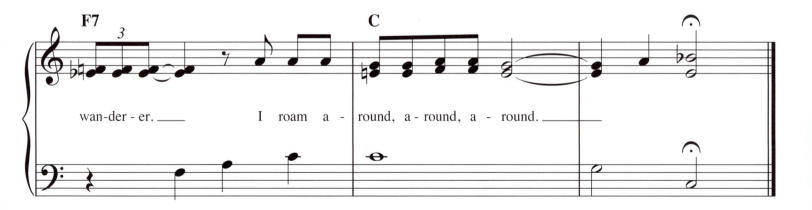

wan - der - er. ___ I roam a - round, a - round, a - round.

WHOLE LOTTA SHAKIN' GOIN' ON

Words and Music by
DAVID WILLIAMS

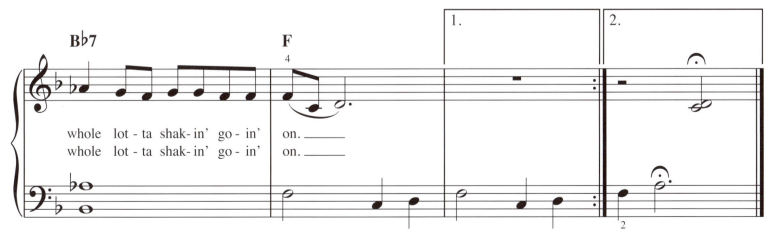

WHY

Words and Music by BOB MARCUCCI
and PETER DeANGELIS

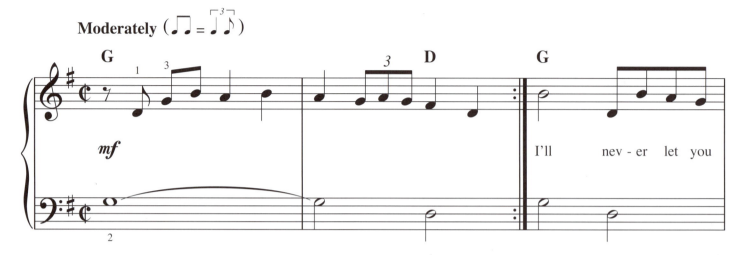

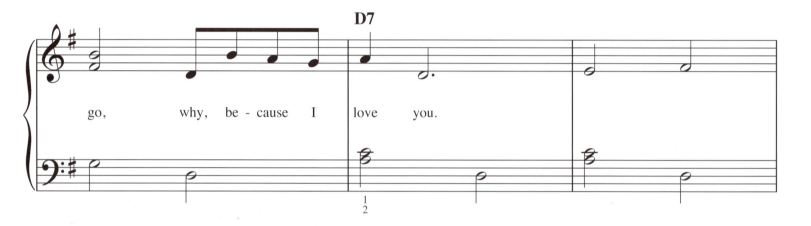

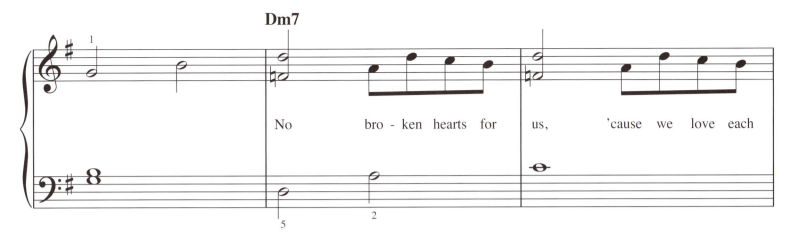

No bro - ken hearts for us, 'cause we love each

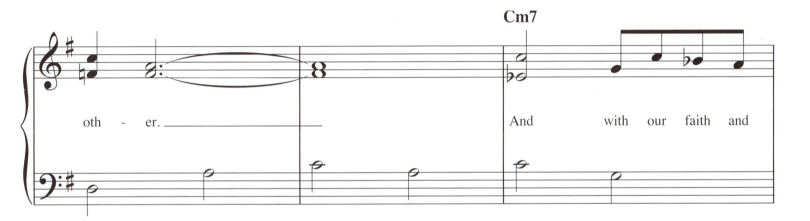

oth - er. _____ And with our faith and

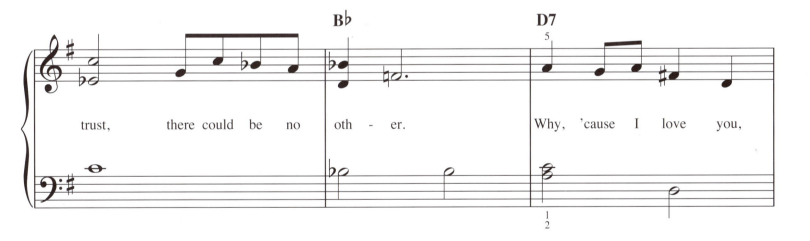

trust, there could be no oth - er. Why, 'cause I love you,

why, 'cause you love me. I think you're aw - f'ly sweet, why, be - cause I

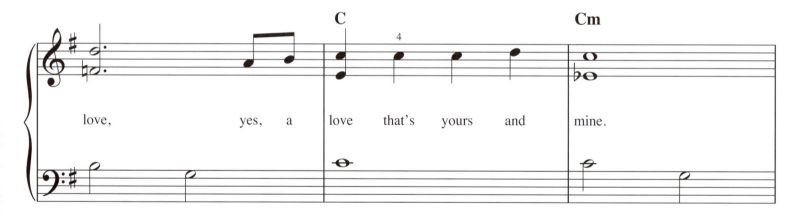

It's Easy to Play Your Favorite Songs with Hal Leonard Easy Piano Books

The Best Praise & Worship Songs Ever

The name says it all: over 70 of the best P&W songs today. Titles include: Awesome God • Blessed Be Your Name • Come, Now Is the Time to Worship • Days of Elijah • Here I Am to Worship • Open the Eyes of My Heart • Shout to the Lord • We Fall Down • and more.
00311312.................................$19.99

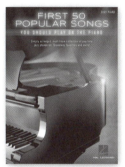

First 50 Popular Songs You Should Play on the Piano

50 great pop classics for beginning pianists to learn, including: Candle in the Wind • Chopsticks • Don't Know Why • Hallelujah • Happy Birthday to You • Heart and Soul • I Walk the Line • Just the Way You Are • Let It Be • Let It Go • Over the Rainbow • Piano Man • and many more.
00131140.................................$16.99

The Greatest Video Game Music

28 easy piano selections for the music that envelops you as you lose yourself in the world of video games, including: Angry Birds Theme • Assassin's Creed Revelations • Dragonborn (Skyrim Theme) • Elder Scrolls: Oblivion • Minecraft: Sweden • Rage of Sparta from God of War III • and more.
00202545.................................$17.99

Jumbo Easy Piano Songbook

200 classical favorites, folk songs and jazz standards. Includes: Amazing Grace • Beale Street Blues • Bridal Chorus • Buffalo Gals • Canon in D • Cielito Lindo • Danny Boy • The Entertainer • Für Elise • Greensleeves • Jamaica Farewell • Marianne • Molly Malone • Ode to Joy • Peg O' My Heart • Rockin' Robin • Yankee Doodle • dozens more!
00311014.................................$19.99

Songs from *A Star Is Born*, *The Greatest Showman*, *La La Land*, and More Movie Musicals

Movie musical lovers will delight in this songbook chock full of top-notch songs arranged for easy piano with lyrics from blockbuster movies. Includes: City of Stars from *La La Land* • Suddenly from *Les Misérables* • This Is Me from *The Greatest Showman* • Shallow from *A Star Is Born* • and more.
00287577.................................$17.99

50 Easy Classical Themes

Easy arrangements of 50 classical tunes representing more than 30 composers, including: Bach, Beethoven, Chopin, Debussy, Dvorak, Handel, Haydn, Liszt, Mozart, Mussorgsky, Puccini, Rossini, Schubert, Strauss, Tchaikovsky, Vivaldi, and more.
00311215.................................$14.99

Pop Songs for Kids

Kids from all corners of the world love and sing along to the songs of Taylor Swift, One Direction, Katy Perry, and other pop stars. This collection features 25 songs from these and many more artists in easy piano format. Includes: Brave • Can't Stop the Feeling • Firework • Home • Let It Go • Shake It Off • What Makes You Beautiful • and more.
00221920.................................$14.99

Simple Songs – The Easiest Easy Piano Songs

Play 50 of your favorite songs in the easiest of arrangements! Songs include: Castle on a Cloud • Do-Re-Mi • Happy Birthday to You • Hey Jude • Let It Go • Linus and Lucy • Over the Rainbow • Smile • Star Wars (Main Theme) • Tomorrow • and more.
00142041.................................$14.99

VH1's 100 Greatest Songs of Rock and Roll

The results from the VH1 show that featured the 100 greatest rock and roll songs of all time are here in this awesome collection! Songs include: Born to Run • Good Vibrations • Hey Jude • Hotel California • Imagine • Light My Fire • Like a Rolling Stone • Respect • and more.
00311110.................................$29.99

River Flows in You and Other Eloquent Songs for Easy Piano Solo

24 piano favorites arranged so that even beginning players can sound great. Includes: All of Me • Bella's Lullaby • Cristofori's Dream • Il Postino (The Postman) • Jessica's Theme (Breaking in the Colt) • The John Dunbar Theme • and more.
00137581.................................$14.99

Disney's My First Song Book

16 favorite songs to sing and play. Every page is beautifully illustrated with full-color art from Disney features. Songs include: Beauty and the Beast • Bibbidi-Bobbidi-Boo • Circle of Life • Cruella De Vil • A Dream Is a Wish Your Heart Makes • Hakuna Matata • Under the Sea • Winnie the Pooh • You've Got a Friend in Me • and more.
00310322.................................$17.99

Top Hits of 2019

20 of the year's best are included in this collection arranged for easy piano with lyrics. Includes: Bad Guy (Billie Eilish) • I Don't Care (Ed Sheeran & Justin Bieber) • ME! (Taylor Swift feat. Brendon Urie) • Old Town Road (Remix) (Lil Nas X feat. Billy Ray Cyrus) • Senorita (Shawn Mendes & Camila Cabello) • Someone You Loved (Lewis Capaldi) • and more.
00302273.................................$16.99

Get complete song lists and more at
www.halleonard.com